In The Midst Of Darkness

The Study of Ghosts

Edward W. Krietemeyer

Dedicated

To my lovely wife Lourdes, and all the years she had to put
up with me.

To my cat Oscar, who takes an interest in me only at
feeding time!

Contents

About the Author
Preface

IN THE MIDST OF DARKNESS

Acknowledgments

RC Design Rick Craft for the photograph used for the cover. rcdesignstudios.com

About the Author

Edward W. Krietemeyer has always had an overwhelming curiosity needing to know how everything works, and how everything worked together. Having no explanation is not an answer. We all have had questions at one time about our existence. What happens when we die, as we get older that question takes on new meaning when the people that were such an important part of our lives start passing away. When looking to medical science for an explanation, it came down to if your heart stopped beating you cease to exist. The more I researched the less critical thinking I found about life after death. Throughout recorded history there has always been the presence described as a Ghost. When I researched religion, the common underlying theme in Christianity is that everyone was going to Hell, and that is from simply following one belief over another. When I started doing research on an afterlife, I was now going to Hell for talking to the dead. Science had closed their minds to the possibility of life after death decades ago labeling Ghosts, and haunted houses as pseudoscience. When I looked at the paranormal field the explanations I was given was based on myth, magick, and mysteries. I started doing my own research in 2006 being critical about how the evidence is collected. To understand how it is even possible, how can I explain it, and how can I recreate it. I have concluded after seven years of asking questions that some small part of our human consciousness can survive death.

Special Acknowledgment

The Institute Of Spectrological Research is an Anomalies Research and Educational Organization established in 2011 to study anomalous audio, and spectrological phenomena based on experimentation, observations, and field research. Educating the public on the unexplained by providing alternative explanations to what people are mistakenly assuming as paranormal. **Taking the Next Best Step.**

Preface

Throughout this book, we will explore everything that is explainable in the paranormal world from equipment that does nothing at all, faking ghostly images, what is evidence, and addressing skeptical explanations. We will explore the science of sound, and analyze data that defies explanation.

What is a Ghost? The biggest problem I have seen in paranormal research is pointing at a phenomenon, and defining it as a Ghost. Well calling anything a ghost when there is no real evidence that a ghost exists is somewhat of a problem, let me explain. Let us say you gathered enough data that point to an unexplained anomaly and that very knowledgeable people agreed, but still have no explanation. There is no explanation because there is not enough data. If there is not enough data then it cannot be defined, as anything more than an anomaly, but if the anomaly is consistent in its observations. Then the anomaly becomes a phenomenon, which is an unexplained observation not a ghost.

You need to discover the source of the phenomenon. So therefore, you need even more data to explain how the phenomenon occurred. If we can explain what caused the phenomena, is that a ghost? No!

There has to be data explaining all the intricacies between the source and the anomaly. The source would need to be more complex than anyone could ever have thought, because if it were anything less it would already be known as a fact of human existence. Even if there was data that showed a connection between the source and the anomaly, what produces the source? Not only do you have to show the research of why the source exists in the first place, but also you would now have to link the anomaly to a once living human being. That in and of itself would require a mountain of data gathered in the strictest of conditions. All methods and procedures in how the data was collected would have to stand up to an onslaught of scrutiny and skeptical review.

Then Medical Science through years of clinical studies must present conclusive evidence that human consciousness can survive death, and must include surviving longer than clinical testing allows. There are ongoing studies researching awareness during clinical death. These studies will investigate reports from patients that claim to have left their body. There must be irrefutable evidence that human consciousness can leave its physical host, and survive indefinitely. This is according to historical accounts and descriptions that has define the human spirit. Realizing that new data explaining new phenomenon would need new terminology that are unique to the discovery would never be defined as a ghost. Traditionally the scientists' that made the discovery would name it. Calling it, a ghost when it is already associated to the field of pseudoscience would bring surmountable ridicule on such research.

How would human consciousness survive without a physical host, as far as Medical Science is concerned there are currently no other means. There has to be data explaining all the intricacies between the source and the anomaly from creation to manifestation. The source would need to be more complex than anyone could ever have thought, because if it were not it would be known as a fact of human existence. There are studies to define human consciousness that are inconclusive.

Then of course taking a leap forward, the source and phenomenon somehow stored the consciousness, but we would have to explain how it could interact with us. All without a physical host. You have to address other theories from parallel universes, particle entanglement or some type of quantum involvement; all would have to be included, or disproved.

Then after all this can we call it a ghost? No!

You must understand extraordinary claims, such as an afterlife. Requires an extraordinary amount of evidence and that is evidence we currently do not have.

Chapter 1

The Search for Human Consciousness

As we learn more about the human brain, we realize how marvelous its complexity. There are ongoing studies in research institutes and colleges all over the world with a single goal of understanding the human mind. There has been a growing interest in the concept of the mind as a conscious form of energy.

In 1994, Dr. Hammeroff and Physicist Sir Roger Penrose put forth a new theory in Consciousness, biology and quantum hypotheses: Inside each brain cell, there are fibrous called microtubules, hollow rods that function primarily to help support and shape the cell. Quantum processes called entanglement believed to play a pivotal role in human consciousness. Quantum effects have been shown to control several biological processes, and when the microtubules die, they lose their quantum state. The quantum information cannot be destroyed it can instead redistribute into our surroundings. Quantum effects can continue outside the body and can exists indefinitely.

In 1998, a collaboration of the medical and scientific world came together forming The Human Consciousness Project with the goal of mapping the gamut of brain activity including the unconscious. Researchers around the world are piecing together what they now call the spectrum of human consciousness. There is already undisputed evidence that such a spectrum of consciousness exists. It is our higher-level cognitive functions that distinguish us from all other species on this planet. An article published by The Human Consciousness Project in 2008 entitled 'The First Few

Minutes After Death' will explore countless accounts of near-death experiences, such occurrences have been dated as far back as ancient Greece, science is now taking serious steps forward to explore the nature of the phenomenon. The three-year AWARE Study aims to determine whether the experience is a physiological event or evidence that human consciousness is far more complicated than we ever believed.

The late Nobel-winning neuroscientist Sir John Eccles, arguing that the human mind and consciousness may in fact constitute a separate, undiscovered anomaly apart from the brain.

Dr. Sam Parnia, an intensive care physician, director of resuscitation research at Stony Brook University School of medicine in New York. Director of the 'Aware Study' researching what happens to human consciousness during and after death.

A proportion of patients describe a sensation of separating from the body and watching doctors and nurses working on them. [His book cites a 2001 case, in which a Dutch patient's dentures were removed during cardiac arrest. When the nurses could not find the dentures later, the patient was able to remind them where they were.] When you stop blood flow to the brain and do CPR, there is no measurable brain function. Therefore, there should be no reports of conscious awareness of people being able to see and hear things. The question becomes, how can people have conscious awareness when they have gone beyond the threshold of death?

Exploration

As I explore what is known about the physiological processes of the human brain. I originally focused on what parts of our brain we cannot put in the ground. My earlier ideas, and I would like to clarify an idea is not a theory. A theory can be tested I am not in the position to test physiological theories. I do not have the expertise, but resources as luck would have it. I been given unfeather access to a couple neurologists, and a physicist.

My original idea was if the capacity of our working and short-term memory the electrochemical processes of our brain could store just one days' worth of memories in its electrochemical memory cells. The part of the brain that we cannot put in the ground would fit most observations. The more I learned about the capacity of the human brain referring to the before mentioned processes that are used to temporarily store, organize and manipulate information only lasts in the brain 20 to 30 seconds at any given moment. Definitely not the long-term solution I was looking for. Remember that at the point of death as our internal organs start to shut down the brain goes into panic mode, euphoria turns into unconsciousness. Death follows over the course of several hours. What I have described is how I know that there are parts missing in the neurological explanations on how the human brain works, or should I say how my neurologist thinks it works. That somehow the whole brain is involved not just a fragment, but everything we once were. Our Human consciousness as described by most neuroscientists. There seems to be a neurological-net that ties the brain together as a whole some believe that net it is the skin of the brain itself, and would be closer to what has been observed. Medical Science once said when we die we simply cease to exist, and yet new medical research is challenging that concept.

AWARE study preliminary results: October 2013

The AWARE study (AWAreness during REsuscitation) is a multi-hospital clinical study of the brain and consciousness during cardiac arrest, including tests of the validity of perceptions during the out-of-body portion of near-death experiences. The latest status is that more data and larger scale studies will probably be required, and an end to the study is not anticipated in the near future. A report of preliminary results from the first five years of the study is likely be presented through a scientific journal or a scientific conference.

This two year clinical study was inconclusive. In all research the quality of the data hinges on the participants. The failure to follow procedures that was intrusted to local staff, and medical professionals reduced years of research to nothing.

Chapter 2

Reality, or Hallucination

Over the past seven years, I have investigated locations that are haunted. Subsequently we end up finding people that are haunted. Although the haunt is from an entirely different reason. The First most commonly reported cases of paranormal occurrences have to do with "Sleep Disorders". A Mental Phenomenon occurs at our threshold of consciousness that is a natural bodily process as we sleep, called REM atonia that results in a paralytic paralysis that prevents us from acting out in our dreams. In some instances, caught in between a sleeping and wakening state. You are aware of the paralysis, which usually passes in a few minutes as you return to full wakefulness in some cases can include visual hallucinations, or strange sensations, such as feeling a distinct foreign presence in the room, seeing shadows, or hearing footsteps. Typically, episodes would occur from a nocturnal awakening, and could happen at any time of the night. Initially, symptoms would occur at random, from weekly, to a month or two apart for the preceding month, events can increase to several times a night. People often report encountering apparition-like entities or other worldly beings including monsters popularly known as "waking dreams" or "night terrors, and has been proposed as an explanation for reports of paranormal activity.

Anxiety Disorders are common psychiatric disorders that effect about 14% of Americans characterized by excessive and abnormal fear based on real or imagined events.

Common Symptoms: (sleep paralysis)

Last night when I was sleeping, I thought I was having a dream, but now I am not so sure, it felt so real. It was as if I was above myself. Lying on my bed I felt as if my wrists and ankles were being held down, something very heavy was on top of me. I tried to move and I tried to yell but I could not. Then, just as I woke up, it was gone and I felt very strange and could hardly breathe. I stayed awake for hours thinking about what it could be.

Sleep terrors: (night terrors)

Sleep terrors are the most disruptive arousal disorder since it may involve loud screams and panic; in extreme cases, it may result in bodily harm or property damage by running about or hitting walls. Unfortunately, all attempts to console the individual are futile and may prolong or intensify the victim's confused state. Usually the victim experiences amnesia after the event but it may not be complete amnesia. **Up to 3% of adults suffer from sleep terrors, and exhibited** behavior of this parasomnia can range from mild to the extremely violent.

Fantasy prone personalities are the cause of the third most reported type of paranormal activity. A fantasy prone person spend a large portion of his or her time fantasizing, have vividly intense fantasies, have paranormal experiences, and often confuse or mix their fantasies with their real memories.

Pseudologia fantastica
In psychiatry, also called mythomania, compulsive lying or pathological lying, is a behavior of habitual or compulsive lying. Pathological lying has been defined as "falsification entirely disproportionate to any discernible end in view. The

individual may be aware they are lying, or may believe they are telling the truth, being unaware that they are relating fantasies.

Exposure to toxins

Carbon monoxide is odorless, colorless, tasteless, and initially a non-irritating toxic gas. Because it is very difficult for people to detect, ($CO2$) can kill you before you are aware it is in your home, and is often mistaken for the flu. These symptoms include headaches, dizziness, disorientation, nausea, and fatigue. Carbon monoxide poisoning can become life threatening in a matter of hours. Testing for Carbon monoxide is critical with the onset of these symptoms.

Long-term exposure to high electromagnetic fields - EMF can cause serious health concerns. Devices that produce high levels of EMF will continue to emit EMFs even when turned off. Household wiring is another source of high EMF exposure; you should hire a qualified electrician to investigate and repair the cause. Symptoms from high EMF exposure are similar to Carbon monoxide poisoning, and can include biological stress, anxiety and depression.

Perception and Reality

Your mind dictates your reality. There is a thin line between a dream, and the world you surrounded yourself in...

What most paranormal teams do not take into account that the biggest cause of Ghost sightings are due to emotional trauma such as a recent bereavement, mourning the death of a loved one or the most common, mental illness? There are unsuspected dangers when it comes to the human mind that best served by a medical professional. Our memories during times of grief or illness are at their strongest. A simple act can trigger memories that can take you to a time when you envision what you expect to see, even if what you are envisioning is no longer there. Then other times it is a matter of assuming or mistaken what seen. It is normal for your brain to fabricate a mental representation for a substituted reality. How our brain deals with processes sensory input, comprises how we perceives the world around us, and a lot of the time that perception is wrong. We see the world around us as stable, even though our sensory input is incomplete, and rapidly changing.

People suffering from <u>Schizophrenia</u> have symptoms ranging from distorted thoughts, feelings of paranoia and hallucinations. They are usually withdrawn or easily agitated, and account for the second most commonly reported cases of paranormal occurrences. Medications can also cause similar symptoms as Schizophrenia make sure the individual that is experiencing unexplained phenomenon consults with a health care professional.

Prescription medications can cause hallucinations, either as a common side effect, which can cause people to believe they are seeing or hearing something that is not there. When encountering someone that is experiencing side effects to have them consult with their doctor to check for health problems.

As paranormal researchers, you should never take the place of a health care professional. Suggesting a course of treatment can aggravate possibly yet unknown health problems not only risking the health of the client as well as opening you up for civil and criminal recourse. Even providing an aspirin to someone can be interpreted in a court of law as practicing medicine without a license.

Visual hallucinations while sitting in the dark

In the dark, the human mind begins to lose its grip, causing test subjects to experience visual and aural hallucinations. A Study done by Psychologist Peter Suedfeld from the University College London said when a group of people is placed in a dark, quiet room, many start hallucinating after just a few minutes. The participants who were not prone to hallucinations started hallucinating after 15 minutes. What we saw for sensory deprivation hallucinations is that when there is no information coming in (the brain), the brain produces an alternate reality of what is supposed to be there, some experiences were reported to be unpleasant. Same thing happens when you take hallucinogenic drugs.

Hallucinations Continued ...

A study that links caffeine to hallucinations, according to Australian researchers at La Trobe University. This study suggested that people that over indulge in caffeinated drinks having more than three cups of coffee at a time would be more prone to hearing voices. There are more than enough conflicting reports about coffee from health concerns to health benefits. In the study, researchers brought a small group of overly caffeinated volunteers to a lab, and had them put on headphones where they listen to white noise, but first suggesting that they would be listening to White Christmas. Now having extensive knowledge to the effects of listening to white noise, and other noise generators in my work with anomalous voice phenomena the continued research of electronic voice phenomena my study on recognizing sound anomalies. Continued listening to white noise in and of itself would be suspect of causing the hallucinations. Then making a suggestion of what you would be hearing while listening to the white noise invalidates the study. If you take anyone caffeinated to the hilt or not and then put headphones on them playing white noise just before suggesting that they would be listening to White Christmas. They are going to hear White Christmas this is the power of suggestion not a hallucination. This study has many flaws, such as controls (how much caffeine), sample size (suggesting only one song tends to sway the results), and small polling size even though the number of participants was left out of the study. In conclusion, there is not enough evidence that caffeine alone could cause severe hallucinations.

Chapter 3

What Is Explainable (Particulate Contamination)

You can easily explain away camera anomalies when it comes to using a flash. The new digital cameras, and their compact size means the flash is closer to the lens illuminating every particle moving past the lens field of view.

Thus the ORB was born.

It is usually the inexperienced paranormal investigator's most prized catch. Is what I, and most everyone in the real world calls DUST.

I have heard every type of explanation of why their ORBs are real spirit ORBs because.

It glowed: Is there a light source, any light source? Your camera cannot record in total darkness unless it is infrared. Infrared is a light source.

It manifested then vanished: the particle merely moved in, and out of the light source.

If you look closely, the spirit ORB has a face in it.

Pareidolia: A psychological phenomenon involving a vague and random stimulus (often an image or sound) perceived as significant.

The below paragraph can help explain the majority of ORBs. The rest are reflections, lens flairs, bugs, and lighting. So if the ORB changes direction, or in one picture, but not the others? This is why.

The air in any room even if the room is sealed is constantly moving. You do not need an open window to have airflow. Simply put; particles move around in static charged clusters of particulate matter be it dust, moisture, plant pollen, and spores. One other point I wanted to make about spores and other particulates is that lighting conditions effect the color, so everyone has a different perspective, and a different perception of what that color is. Temperature changes create convection currents that continuously circulate the air in every room. Hot air rises, and cold air falls, but there is more to this story. The hot air molecules, as they rise pushes against other air molecules that move out of the way causing some air molecules to cool, or heat up depending on walls, windows, and other surfaces causing continuously changing currents of air.

One of the arguments I have heard repeatedly about ORBs is that it cannot be dust because I had the place cleaned. Human beings are the biggest cause of the particulate contamination in the first place if there was only one person in the room. How much particle contamination can one person produce in just **one hour**?

The human body made up of around 10 trillion cells. Your skin makes up about 16 percent of your body weight, which means you have roughly 1.6 trillion skin cells according to a person's size. Of those billions of skin cells, between **30,000 and 40,000 of them fall off every hour**. Over a 24-hour period, you lose almost a million skin cells.

Perspiration (sweat) exuded through the pores of the skin to the surface has a cooling effect due to latent heat (heat released by the body) in the evaporation of moisture. The skin secretes salts, water, and an oily/waxy substance, called **sebum**, to lubricate and waterproof the surface of your skin and hair.

Excretion through sweat glands is the process by which waste products of metabolism and other surplus substances that may have a lethal effect eliminated from an organism, and must therefore excreted. This includes nitrogen compounds, water, CO_2, phosphates, and sulfates. Our maximum sweat rates of an adult can be up to **2-4 liters per hour** or 10-14 liters per day.

Hair everyone loses between 40 and 120 strands a day, depending on how much hair you have, your age and your hair's growth cycle. People with fine hair tend to have more of it and therefore will lose more of it than their thicker-haired sisters and brothers. Your hair also thins, as you get older, particularly after menopause for women while aging men experience thinning. **(1.6 to 5 strands of hair per hour)**

Breathing is the process that moves air in and out of the lungs. In addition to removing carbon, dioxide and other waste gases. Breathing results in loss of water from the body. Exhaled air has a relative humidity of 100% because of water diffusing across the moist surface of breathing passages and alveoli.

Adults lose nearly two to three quarts (12 cups or 2.8 liters) of water every day through the process of breathing. Although estimates may vary due to changes in climate, or increased activity. **(1/2 cup or 0.11 liters of water by breathing per hour)**

Microscopic Parasites the most common are dust mites that inject skin-dissolving saliva into their host and consume the liquefied skin. Of course, dust mites because their microscopic cast skins and feces are one of the causes of airborne allergens. One dust mite is 200 to 400 microns in length and at any given time there are tens of thousands, to tens of millions living off you, right now!

You may not have realized, but the above statistics are describing the amounts of particulates generated from one "*naked*" human being. If we were to add clothes, the list of contaminants from clothing alone would run off the page into the abyss. From our surrounding environment, and lifestyle we expose ourselves to food particles, pet hair/dandruff, and building materials a lot of which are the components of dust such as concrete, and plaster. Particulates generated from any material when disturbed, and if the materials were in a state of deterioration, there would be a concentration of that particular type of airborne particulate. Finally yet importantly contaminants from outside in the air that are brought in with you, dirt, plant pollen, spores, fungi, and other man made pollutants.

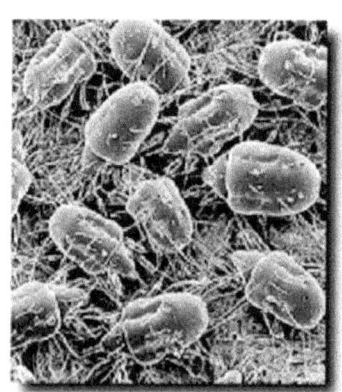

Dust is mostly composed of dead skin cells, dessicated corpses of dust mites that eat the dead skin cells, and their feces. Building materials such as plaster, fibers from clothing, and other man made pollutants.

The other argument I have heard was; it cannot be dust because I have HEPA - (High-Efficiency Particulate Air) filters installed. There is a presumption that all particulates in the air would be removed? Filters meeting the HEPA standard must remove 99.97% of all particles greater than 0.3 micron from the air that passes through it, again from the air that passes through the filter. This would greatly depend on how efficient the ventilation system is at the location. Then again if we compared it to a semiconductor manufacturer clean room that has a low-level of environmental pollutants such as dust, airborne microbes, aerosol particles and chemical vapors. That classified in terms of the number and sizes of particles suspended in its atmosphere according to ISO - 14644-1 cleanroom standards. To illustrate, in a Class 100 cleanroom, a cubic foot of air allowed only having 100 particles whose size is 0.5 micron. A particle defined as a solid or liquid object between 0.001 and 1000 microns in size. I wanted to emphasize that even in the cleanest rooms in the world there is still particulate contamination.

The nearest thing to a human Spirit in a ORB, are the **dead skin cells** that came from you, and everyone else that had passed through the room that makes up DUST...

Insects: Are mistaken for fairies, spirit ORBs, Ghosts, and Angels. Bug are very colorful and highly luminescent that little green, or blue ORB as it buzzed bye, and depending on the cameras shutter speed can make bright streaks. Moths have been mistaken for ORB and Angels depending on how out of focus they are. Grasshoppers in flight with their legs extended look like little people with wings, yep fairies! Insects crawling across the lens of a camera looks like a blurry moving apparition. Which gives the illusion that a Ghost is walking through the room, but was only a bug moving across the lens.

Rods 'skyfish': Is it an Angel or anxious Moths? Philip Callahan, an entomologist while working with the U.S. Department of Agriculture in the 1970s. Callahan discovered that the infrared light spectrum emitted by a candle flame happens to contain a few of the exact same frequencies of light given off by female moths' pheromones, or sex hormones. Callahan had previously discovered that the pheromones are luminescent they glow very faintly. Along with slow shutter speeds creates these trails that been called rods by "paranormal enthusiast". Insect beat their wings roughly 10 times per second anything longer than 1/2 second exposure when in motion starts to become transparent. The body of the insect is relatively solid while in flight. The wings create a motion blur as it moves past the lens of the camera resulting in an elongated object with a wavy structure down the length of the body from the insect beating its wings.

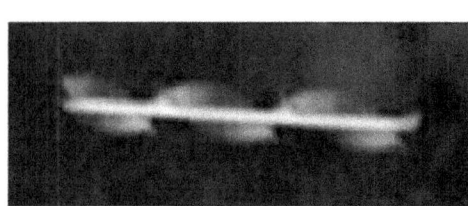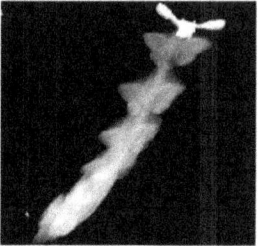

Shadows: Two-dimensional shadows come from three-dimensional objects such as yourself, and everything else. We live in a three dimensional world you should expect to see two-dimensional shadows everywhere. Whenever you think something is paranormal, you need to ask yourself; Is what I have experienced reproducible, or explainable?

What Is Explainable (No Spirits Necessary!)

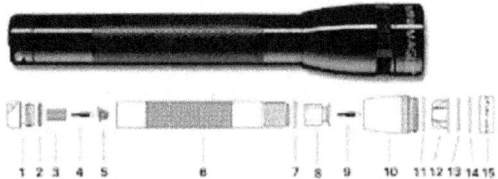

Mini-Maglite Flashlight Trick (xenon lamp)
Note: The new LED Mag-LITEs' do not heat up, so the trick does not work for them.

We have all seen the Mag-LITE trick used by paranormal groups. I am going to explain how it works. It is simply a short circuit just like bad wiring. They adjust the lamp reflector housing #10 until the xenon lamp turns on! The lamp starts to heat up and expands the pressure switch #8 in the lamp reflector housing #10 **Light goes off!**
You can see the lamp dim just before it goes out.
This is a good time to ask that paranormal question.

As soon as the lamp is, off! The reflector housing #10 starts to cool down contracting the pressure switch #8 until it reconnects the circuit. **Light goes on!**

It is a very consistent on, off!
Now ask a question and wait for the light to turn itself either off, or on! Anyone can do it...

It does not matter how many Mag-LITEs' you use if the light is off, as it cools down it will reconnect turning back on, and if the light is on it will heat up until disconnecting.

The Mag-LITE is operating like a heat engine. Expansion and contraction is what is driving the light to turn on, and off according to the laws of thermodynamics.

Scratches: Most scratches are self-inflicted often while we are sleeping. I have done it dozens of times nothing paranormal about it. The reason there is three marks is because you have three longer fingers on your hand the pinky or little finger rarely leaves a mark do to size and strength most of us are unaware how often we scratch ourselves. It is only after scratches become slightly infected they turn red, and you start feeling a burning sensation. This is from the body's natural defense of inflammation, and from fighting off infection, it is very normal.

A growing number of smart phone applications that claim to detect Ghosts. Smart phones have a variety of sensors all of which are useless for ghosts hunting. The newer iphone has a built in magnetometer used to detect EM fields, and then your cell phone would still be useless because most magnetometer are calibrated for AC, and since we do not know what ghosts are made of. We do know for sure that they are not alternating current because AC is manmade. If that does not stop you from bringing your cell phone, maybe contaminating the environment will. Cell phones produce microwaves, and radio waves, and are constantly accepting calls, voice mail notifications, and text messages unless you turn them off! These apps are cheap and now the disclaimer; the app is purely aimed for those looking to trick others or have a little fun, and should be used for entertainment purposes only. Most all the applications for your smart phone uses a software algorithm like Ghost Radar to make all the bells, and whistles go off, and does nothing at all to detect ghosts.

I have no problem with people playing with toys. It is when they use these toys on real investigations in people's homes, and claim it as evidence without knowing the difference.

Ideomotor Effect is a psychological phenomenon wherein a subject makes motions unconsciously. William B. Carpenter coined the term "ideomotor action" in 1852 in his explanation for the movements of rods and pendulums by dowsers, and some table turning or lifting by spirit mediums (the ones that were not accomplished by cheating). Carpenter argued that muscular movement could be initiated by the mind independently of volition or emotions. We may not be aware of it, but suggestions made to the mind by others or by observations. Those suggestions can influence the mind and affect motor behavior.

Dowsing Rod's: Two metal rods bent on the ends at a 45-degree angle held loosely and allowed to swing from side to side …believing that once they cross a spirit is present. *(Ideomotor Effect)*

Pendulum: Pendulum Dowsing is once again unconscious involuntary movement causing the Pendulum on the chain to swing or rotate freely over a chart, or an Ouija Board. *(Ideomotor Effect)*

 **Ouija Board:** Also known as a spirit board or talking board, is a flat board marked with the letters of the alphabet, the numbers 0-9, the words 'yes' 'no' 'hello' and 'goodbye', and other symbols and words are sometimes also added to help personalize the board. It is a registered trademark of Hasbro Inc. *(Ideomotor Effect)*

Many devices based entirely on subjective reality. This is a psychological phenomenon involving a vague and random stimulus perceived as meaningful 'audio pareidolia'. One of these devices a broken radio called a **"Ghost Box – Spirit Box – Frank's Box – Radio Shack Hack!"** How it works is by skipping along through radio broadcasts picking up random clearer stations along with that word or two that is believed to be significant to the question asked. Most of these pieces of equipment that sells for hundreds of dollars detect nothing but RF contamination. There is usually a disclaimer written into the documentation or on the device itself, for entertainment purposes only!

Laser Grid: The pen was never designed to be on all the time. A collar forces the button down keeping the laser on which results in the laser overheating. Along with rapid power drainage creating fluctuations in the beam (ripples) that are mistaken as anomalous activity.

EMF Pumps and EM Vortex Pumps: These devices created to produce alternating electromagnetic fields to feed your ghost making the activity that is associated with Ghosts stronger. I have built an EM Pump, but got a different effect. On one investigation, I mounted the EM Pump on the cameras tripod. You can hear something walk up to it stayed there for a while started talking completely unseen as if it was curious. Then went downstairs and scared the researcher as it walked up to her.

Ionizers: Another feed your ghost idea it creates a static charge in the air to mimic an electrical storm. The idea is that paranormal activity increases during storms. The only true substantiated use of these devices is to reduce the amount of dust in the room 'less Orbs' but serves no other purpose.

FLIR thermal camera systems is a very expensive piece of equipment when I first saw it on a paranormal non-reality TV show capturing incredible evidence. I said to myself that I have to have one. These cameras can start a little over thousand dollars the camera used on that show cost $15,000 what I learned was that it is incapable of reading temperature from the air itself. It is specifically designed to look through the air for a reflective surface. Such as an Infrared laser thermometer that can only pick up surface temperature. The ghost by all descriptions should not have surface or mass then the FLIR would not pick it up.

Infrared laser thermometer can only pick up surface temperatures and cannot track cold or hot spots unless it has a temperature probe to check for free flowing ambient air.

Ovilus I, I-phone app, I-Ovilus, Ovilus III, and so on…a creation by Digital Dowsing. Bill Chappell has never claim that it can do anything at all. The Ovilus consumer makes most of the claims. It is not possible to build a device that detects or communicates with ghosts, because no one, and I mean no one in the entire world, has any idea how to prove that ghosts exist, let alone how they communicate. It links magnetic frequencies to a list of words. On another reincarnation of the Ovilus, it is possible to modify the list, and if you have not seen this, enough in this book the disclaimer. "For Entertainment Purposes Only"

Kirlian photography is a process of laying object on a photographic plate and passing electricity through it, which results in an ethereal looking photo. The "aura" is moisture that is stimulated by the electrical charge. When the same process done in a vacuum, no aura appears.

What Is Explainable (Camera Anomalies)

Is the world a picture, No it is not! The world is flowing, moving, constantly changing; we adapt and change with it. A picture can only capture life, while video captures living.

EXIF (EXchangeable Image Format)
Extensions to image file formats that hold the camera settings used to take the picture. Developed in 1995 by JEIDA for JPEG images, EXIF data was added to TIFF, RAW and other formats later. Most digital cameras support EXIF and save the data in the file headers. However, when an image is edited, the software may automatically remove the EXIF data. EXIF reader, which is a utility that used to read, display and save EXIF data from a file.

The first and most common explanation for a Ghost, beside the Orb is camera anomalies caused by long exposure. Anything over 1/2 second exposure or shutter malfunction, anything moving in front of the lens including people becomes transparent. If you are using night scene on your camera stop unless you use a tripod. When you have something, you do not understand happen with your digital camera look at the original photo as it came from the camera. Look at the EXIF file and it will tell you what camera settings were in place. You may find out why your camera malfunction took place. Most camera anomalies are explainable, and can be avoided by checking the camera settings for lighting conditions with the use of a tripod when taking images in low light for long exposures. Lens hoods can reduce the amount of dust 'Orbs' in your images, and will help protect the lens from adverse weather conditions.

Motion blurs or double exposures can cause people to look transparent or double image. This is another camera setting error. The image taken during the day or in a well-lit room with the camera set for long exposure with or without the use of a flash.

Light trails or Streamers are elongated streaks of light caused by long exposure, and any light source or reflective surface while in motion traveling through or reproduced throughout the image. It would be unlikely that anyone would have seen anything unusual at the time the picture was taken, and you can say that about any camera anomaly.

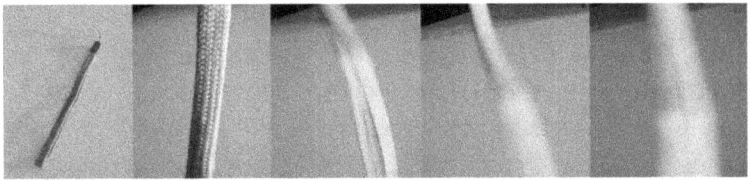

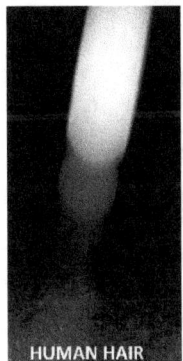

HUMAN HAIR

Then you have the 'vortex' or what I like to call the camera strap or human hair caught in front of the lens. An example to the left appears as one or more streaks of light.

Mist: changes in humidity can cause a white 'mist' to appear in a picture. Breath is 100% moisture that appear again as a white 'mist'. Then there is smoke, and smokers breath. **Smoke** has a blue tint while you can tell if the person breathing is a smoker, or non-smoker because the smokers breath has a brown tint commonly mistaken for a manifesting ghost by the more novus paranormal enthusiast. It really does not take a big difference in temperature to cause a mist a lot of time the mist might not even be visible to the naked eye until illuminated by the camera flash. Wet or damp foliage and as little as a 5-degree temperature difference with the proper barometric pressure can also cause mist.

Optical artifacts are inherent imperfections in the optics of all cameras. Ghosts exist in photography caused by an internal reflection in the lens itself looking like another mist although the reflection reduces the frequency in the light source turning the mist a different colors, and is usually directly opposite of a strong light source. One other cause of mists and are the most overlooked, are the contaminants that can end up on the lens itself from fingerprints, dust, and dirt. A smudges on the lens can look like mist. The solution is to clean the camera lens often.

Lens Flair or Glare is a scattering from any light source such as the Sun, the Moon, and fire. Fire especially with the fluctuation of the light source can make the anomaly move around, and has been mistaken for Angels, and Ghosts.

Example of
Lens Flair

Ghost Cell Camera Applications for both iPhone Android: New ones come out every Halloween in the spirit of the season to frighten the unaware. It's one of the most annoying parts about the paranormal field today is people being fooled, or trying to pass off one of these Ghostly Specters. I have even seen paranormal teams trying to pass off a Ghost App image as evidence.

Phone Applications like: Ghost Capture, Ghost Cam, Ghosted, and Ghost Snap to name a few. These apps offer over 50 spirit and ghost images along with the ability to change the transparency levels of the ghosts. This enables them to blend seamlessly into the photo.

I had a CEO of a company call me seeing a picture of a ghostly apparition in the office standing beside a couple employees. I had him send me the picture. It turned out to be another Ghost Camera App image like the ones above. You know it is not a good idea to mess with the CEO, go find someone that cannot fire you.

Computer Generated Photographic Ghosts

Adobe® Photoshop® professional photo editor you can use tools such as **Motion Blur** and move layers of the image in opposite directions to create that Ghostly effect. You know if the person that created the apparition had ever seen a real Ghost they might be able to reproduce it. Then again, the real thing is rare, and fakes are easily recognizable.

Computer Generated Video Ghosts

Most inexpensive video editing software includes 'Green Screen Special Effects' also known as 'Chroma Key Effects.' The green screen is used to introduce a recorded image in front of the screen with let's say someone walking around with a sheet over them, by adjusting the chroma key effect you can add and then fade the length of the footage in the segment just enough to give it that ghostly appearance.

Then of course there is Pepper's ghost an illusionary technique discovered by Scientist and Scholar Giambattista Della Porta in his work of 1584, and the effect was first used successfully by John Pepper in the theatre production of Charles Dickens's *'The Haunted Man'*. Everyone has seen this effect used in the Haunted House at Disneyland. It is simply a reflection on the glass. The image takes on a transparent appearance. Take a picture of the glass, and you have your ghost. People have been faking ghosts since the advent of photography.

Here Mary Todd Lincoln wife of President Abraham Lincoln after his death had this picture taken by a spiritualist photographer.

What Is Explainable (Crossing Over Explored)

There are paranormal groups, and the clairvoyant that have claimed to cross spirits of the dead over to the next realm. Some of the paid haunts take it so seriously that they have wording in the rules, and releases not to cross their spirits over. Some claim the spirits are lost and need help to cross. I have always been curious about the whole crossing over part, and had numerous questions such as,

1. Crossing over to where, exactly?
2. If the spirit crosses and it is too warm there, can the spirit cross back?
3. What are the rituals involved in this crossing?
4. How do you know if the spirit crossed?
5. Finally yet importantly, does the spirit have to go?

I have never had much luck getting answers to these questions, until recently while browsing the internet. I came across a link to a blog about ghost hunting. I am always interested in reading what other teams are doing. Just from the equipment used and evidence collected can speak volumes about the team. While reading the blog I came across a conversation about evidence review. The blogger mention how they crossed some spirits over. Playing the novus, I asked my first question.

Q: I am confused where are the spirits crossing over too? Do the spirits know where they are going after the "crossing"? Why do the spirits need your help?

A: There are many different belief systems out there, so I will attempt to answer this without offending anyone. From my experience and from the communications I have received though my investigations, people are supposed to cross over when they die. Where do they cross over too?

There are many beliefs about this as well. Some call it Heaven; others believe it is just another dimension. Either way, they are supposed to move on. The ones who choose to stay behind tend to be very unhappy. Homeowners will have items moved around their houses; have doors slam, or other activity. During our investigation, we often get direct cries for help. Some of them seem to get lost and need help finding their way. We have several talented psychics we work with who help us with this. They are able to communicate with them and help them find their way. Afterwards, the homes are quiet and the activity diminishes.

Q: So this is a ritual process, or does the psychic tell the spirit to leave, go into the light? You know they crossed, when it is calm, or is there more of an event? Can they come back after crossing?

It is an interesting subject.

A: I find it fascinating as well. The psychic medium does most of what they do quietly. It depends on how the person typically work. They simply have a conversation with the spirit and convince them to move on. Sometimes it works and sometimes it does not. It just depends on whether or not the spirit wants to pass. Afterwards, if it worked it is very quiet and the activity ceases. If it does not work and it is a disruptive, negative spirit, then the measures become more aggressive and they force it to leave.

Q: The forcing to leave part is that a ritual of some type, such as a blessing, cleansing, or something more severe? If that does not work, then what Move!

A: For the negative entities, one psychic called on members of her coven (she is also a witch) to do a banishing ritual.

Another one used a group of mediums to form an energy circle to force the anomaly to leave.

After reading all of this, I feel comfortable in saying that the paid haunts have absolutely nothing to worry about unless you believe in witches and mysticism that is. Then again, you also have to believe that ghosts not only exist, but magick has some influence over them. It would also be a good idea to embrace the concepts of heaven, and hell so there would be some place to cross over too.

Then there is that one other problem that has become more and more apparent, and that if the paid haunt is haunted at all or just made up stories meant to capitalize on the current fad.

Chapter 4

Using EMF meters in Ghost Hunting

One of the questions I have had over the past couple years is why EMF meters are used? What evidence is there that Ghosts emit, manipulate, or disturb electromagnetic fields? There are quite a few unsubstantiated reports that EMF meters 'spike' during paranormal activity, but I cannot find any formal studies, or research that is supported by evidence. It is common to find paranormal enthusiasts using EMF meters in alleged haunted locations to detect fluctuations in the electromagnetic field, without realizing that the world around them are inundated with those very electromagnetic waves. The question that is infrequently asked is can an EMF meter even capable of detecting such fields at all when there is no solid proof that this being exists. So how then is the off the shelve EMF meters calibrated for that purpose? All EMF meters are calibrated from the manufacturer for detecting standard household currents used for the intended purpose of testing for bad wiring. Most all of these other devices have been developed for the paranormal field all of which have unsubstantiated claims of detecting, or communicating with Ghosts, and while there is a whole number of more laughable devices. The focus of this chapter will be limited to the use of EMF meters in the paranormal field. In the early Ghost Hunter's reality, TV show seen the first use of EMF meters as a communication device. The Lutron 822-A Digital and K-II EMF meters, both monitors a range of 50/60 Hz, which is standard AC power. The Mel-8704 specifications list a monitoring range (Super-low frequency) SLF between 30Hz-300Hz. There are many natural sources of (electromagnetic field) EMF that can cause spikes in low field areas from both electrical and non-electrical sources, which cannot be easily distinguished with an EMF meters.

We are all familiar with the crackle of a static electric charge, and the painful reminder of the discharge that occurs after coming in contact with a ground. Then there is the static cling of fabrics just after being removed from the dryer. If you are measuring the electric component of a field, as some meters can, you will find it is very sensitive to static electricity. Static electric charges are extremely common having devices calibrated to detect magnetic fields can produce a 'spike' simply by moving pass it. Just because something is unexplained simply does not mean that you should jump to the conclusion that it is paranormal without first looking for a reasonable explanation for the cause. You should have a complete understanding on how each piece of equipment functions, and what its purpose. What, if any, studies done to show valid evidence from its use? The paranormal field is awash with overpriced equipment with absolutely no substantiated evidence, that it does anything at all.

So how is it that the developers for these unproven gadgets know more about what a Ghost is? When the rest of the world is still trying to figure it out? Should we focus on direct current since human beings do not produce an alternating electromagnetic field? All electronic toys we use today are DC direct current including the digital watch on my wrist. The laptop computer I am using to write this chapter. The Cell phone in my pocket all powered by direct current. In fact, if you walk around your house and looked at all the electronic devices (coffee maker, microwave oven, clock, television, stereo, etc...), you would notice that almost every single one requires a conversion from AC power to DC power before its use. The primary purpose of alternating current AC is because it able to-be magnetically inducted, thus pushed through a step up transformer and then transmitter over long distances at 500,000 volts or more, then stepped back down for distribution to consumers. The major reason why the wall outlet is AC and is converted to DC inside your electronic device is the cost of transportation. It is much cheaper to send AC voltage and step up step down than it is to send DC voltage. Direct current is very useful in batteries, but batteries can generally only provide relatively low-voltage DC power. Many devices need more power to function properly than DC can provide. Most consumer electronics are designed to run on the 120-volt AC power supplied to homes in the way of alternating current or AC, which constantly changes polarity, sending current one way through the circuit, then reversing and sending it the other way. It does this very quickly 50/60 times per second from most American power grids. AC power works well at high voltages, and can be 'stepped up' in voltage by a transformer more easily than direct current.

There is no denying that haunts exist; people have reported experiencing the strange to the very unusual. Many reports of Ghost are the cause of near sleep paralysis very few are unexplainable. Mental Illness and various medications can cause hallucinations that may manifest in a variety of forms. Various forms of hallucinations affect different senses, sometimes occurring simultaneously, creating multiple sensory hallucinations for those experiencing them. I am not saying the unexplainable does not occur it just occurs less often with something as rare as an apparition being in the lowest majority. Over the last seven years my researchers and I have captured audio and video of all manner of occurrences, is it a Ghost? We do not know. Most people assume that it is a Ghost. To date there is no proof that a Ghost is the cause of any haunting. In retrospect, there is more fantasy, than facts in the paranormal circus; from the failure of understanding the equipment to the other causes for EMF spikes, and from what we know about false positives from the K-II it begs the question of why anyone would use an EMF meter at all.

Taking baseline readings in and of itself is pointless data unless the data logged continuously for 24 hours, and then all you would learn at the location is that the electromagnetic field would continuously fluctuate as appliances with timing relays turned themselves off and on. The only valid purpose for an EMF meter would be to detect high levels of EMF that can cause a variety of health problems. EMF Sensitivity is a condition wherein a person or animal is sensitive to the effects of high levels of electromagnetic energy. Everyone is sensitive to these fields to a degree, though some are more so than others are. Some individuals are sensitive to electromagnetic fields. Symptoms of EMF sensitivity include nervousness, skin irritation, headache, anxiety, paranoia, or nausea after prolonged exposure to these places report feelings of "being watched" the effect often gives rise to sincere but unsubstantiated claims of a haunting. Prolonged exposure to high-levels EMF (or short-term exposure with extreme sensitivity) can also lead to drastic mood changes and hallucinations. Any confined or localized area with unhealthy high levels of electromagnetic radiation due to the presence of a large amount of electrical devices, unshielded electrical cables, or power junctions. To date no other EMF meters are equipped with a temperature probe other than the Mel-8704. The device has both a magnetometer for detecting EMF, and an ambient temperature probe to detect room or localized temperature. Which is useful for calculating the seed of sound and distance from reflective surfaces for debunking purposes?

Chapter 5

The Science behind the Research

"Science works on the frontier between knowledge and ignorance its not afraid to admit what we do not know there is no shame in that. The only shame is to pretend we have all the answers."   ~ Neil deGrasse Tyson COSMOS 2014

The idea behind any experiment is to gain some insight into what the anomaly is actually capable of, and by documenting the event as it happens can lead to our understanding of how and why these things occur. The experiment some of which are located in this book is to try, and answer some of the basic questions we all have. Like how can they see, without eyes? If they can see, then what do they see, and to what level can they see? How can they talk without lungs, and vocal cores? How can they move objects without a physical presence? How can they touch without hands? How intelligent are they?

Scientific study requires systematic observation, measurement, and experimentation, and the formulation, testing, and modification of hypotheses.

The first part of any experiment is the question, and there is no shortage of questions. How do you decide on what experiment to do really depends on where you are planning to conduct them. Some locations are better suited for conducting certain types of experiments depending on the haunt. There are locations where the anomaly was very consistent with their responses. We did our dimensional state of being experiment at such a location. Other locations have aggressive and intelligent responses. We did our cognitive experiments at such a location. Remember your results shapes your hypothesis leading to more experimentation that can take your original idea in new directions. In science, being wrong is allowed if we had all the answers there would not be the question, and no need to look.

Scientific Method

What is the Scientific Method? You see many paranormal groups claiming their scientific based, or follow scientific methods, but what does it mean? In the scientific field, everything starts with a question. The reason why it starts with a question is that we do not have an answer to an observation. You will need to collect more data looking for a pattern to form a hypothesis. It's a little more than sitting around in the dark hunting Ghosts. The reason why we know little to nothing about this phenomenon is that big money is not in it. I am surprised that we spend 12.9 million a year for the past fifty years looking for extraterrestrial intelligence, but they draw a line at actually seeing an Alien. Once you made your observations, and collected your data. It is time for the hypothesis. Your hypothesis has to form conclusions based on your data. Now you have to test the validity of your hypothesis by carrying out experiments that can prove the conclusions in your hypothesis. The experiment has to have one or more conditions with independent methods of validating your results. Because your results shapes your hypothesis that leads to more questions, and new experiments, and ultimately your theory based upon a hypothesis, and backed by evidence. Again, after all of that your theory can still be wrong. Science is self-correcting because of new experiments, or observations. Theories are changed, or thrown out in light of new data. Your data, evidence, and methods subjected to skeptical peer review. Peer Review is a method of self-regulation by qualified members of a profession within the relevant field. You should question everything claims abound in this field look for case studies, how was it tested, what research was done, who made the claim, what established parameters used to define what a ghost is, and what evidence was collected.

It is when a politician can win a Nobel Prize for a presentation without doing any of the actual hands on research. That its only purpose is to promote the flawed science in a political agenda. Then there is the need to get government out of science. Government grants favor those scientists whose research reflects political guidelines, or scientists touting a political policy that serves more of a monetary agenda instead of benefiting all of humanity.

I have seen the video of an experiment to test battery drainage that took place at an alleged haunted location. It used a lantern style flashlight that had an ohmmeter attached to the battery there was a Mel -8704 next to it with two or more cameras recording it. Later anomalous activity started as the on flashlight started moving. Even though there was not any noticeable drop on the ohmmeter showing battery drainage. The Mel-8704 showed both temperature change of an increase of 10-degrees, and a spike in the EM field of six Milligauss. Now this evidence showed a correlation between anomalous EMF spikes and temperature change. It would then be reasonable to generate a hypothesis as to what is causing the anomalous reactions based on credible evidence. Even though this was exciting data, there was a problem with credibility. The evidence I just described was from one of those paranormal non-reality TV shows known for staging evidence. Even though the person that overseen the experiment, I would trust unfortunately once someone involved on the show is caught staging evidence it reflects badly on everyone else, and on the evidence I just described.

Skeptical Review

"If you're only skeptical, then no new ideas make it through to you. You never learn anything. You become a crotchety misanthrope convinced that nonsense is ruling the world. (There is, of course, much data to support you.) Since major discoveries in the borderlines of science are rare, experience will tend to confirm your grumpiness. However, every now and then a new idea turns out to be on the mark, valid and wonderful. If you are too resolutely and uncompromisingly skeptical, you are going to miss (or resent) the transforming discoveries in science, and either way you will be obstructing understanding and progress. Mere skepticism is not enough."

~ Carl Sagan THE DEMON-HAUNTED WORLD

While critical thinking presupposes a willingness to examine all sides of an argument. Peer review process is the evaluation of work from associates with equal or similar levels of competence, and constitutes a form of self-regulation by qualified members. Sighting only related articles, and studies that draw a conclusion within a relevant field of research. When skepticism embraced as a blind belief, it becomes the greatest enemy of truth. It's when skeptical believers are confronted with real evidence that challenges their belief system they are struck deaf and blind unable to see or hear anything. Then post unrelated articles that based on mental illnesses for vindication, and when others can confirm what is being seen, and heard. They claim it is merely a hallucination, and pressure others into silence, so not to challenge their explanation, or just scream pseudoscience to avoid producing anything to refute the evidence altogether.

My team has done single blind studies of electronic voice phenomena for the past five years. Therefore, we knew from the results of over 500 participants. What could be heard too what was heard, but when submitting evidence to a group of skeptics expecting to be taken seriously by simply not turning up the volume was able to say they heard nothing at all. An important two-year study from the University of Vigo Spain was ignored leading them to the conclusion that no proof was possible. Realizing they had no technical experience in sound analysis when looking for peer review groups the criticisms meant to point out flaws in assessing the data, and not meant to dismiss the work out of hand.

Arguing for logic, not for truth

Sometimes in the attempt to educate, comments are misinterpreted as an argument when it was initially meant to point out a common error. It has been my experience that there are two initial outcomes. The first is acceptance; the individual realizes that indeed a mistake been made, with some replying in appreciation for the correction, or the response might be a correction in the initial analysis, or more information about some conditions as a way to validate the original statement. There can be constructive well-rounded arguments that is meant to come to a conclusion, not to place blame.

Then we have the second type of response, which is the most common unfortunately. The individual felt confronted with their own ignorance, and immediately became defensive lashing out with derogatory statements. Even if the comment were meant to be informative. There are the few that cannot help themselves but to use non-constructive arguments that only beliefs and fanciful conclusions are accepted. When coming across anyone that does not agree. What better than techniques that they learned in grade school, name-calling!

Really, these people believe so much in fantasies that I have to step back in wonder how they ever made it this far in their lives. It is beyond me how some people can so easily dismissed logic? Society must bend over backwards to cater to these people; I guess most might assume that they have a mental problem, or that they must have a disability where they need special care? In all actuality to say these fantasy prone individuals are stupid is an affront to stupid people everywhere.

Occasionally I come across an article that asks the question. After all these years with thousands of paranormal teams, collecting data. Why then is there no credible proof that ghost exist?

Well even if there was, enough data that can prove ghosts exist. The ghost-hunting enthusiasts are not the type of researchers you would want. Collecting data correctly requires rigorous disciplines something the ghost-hunting enthusiast is not willing to do. Simply put they are just not in it for the data, or the real work that is involved. I have had members in my own team mentioned that doing research "the correct way" took the fun out of the paranormal. When the primary focus is scaring one another in the dark, or bolstering evidence that in the real world means nothing at all. I have yet seen anyone in the paranormal community that has the slightest clue on how to preserve the integrity of the data. It is unrealistic to presume that no credible evidence is possible. The truth is that there would need to be an unbelievable amount of evidence from medical science to, documented correlations between a once living human being, and anomalous voice phenomenon. Verifying the data through personal information from AVP responses against historical documentation, and finally referring to family or loved ones by name.

Chapter 6

What is Evidence in the Paranormal Field

What is evidence, in the paranormal field is something that can provide an explanation supporting a claim or belief. We can capture unexplained activity, but the fundamental purpose for paranormal investigator is to give logical real world explanations for what is being experienced. Not to prove a location is haunted! Begin by documenting everything starting with the claims of activity, interview witnesses then schedule a meeting with the owner to walk around, and photograph the property. It is vital to create an accurate layout of the property including floor plans. Floor plans play a pivotal part in the investigation, and used in pre-investigation briefings, equipment deployment, and most importantly can help debunk evidence. There was a case where we investigated an airplane hangar where every sound from the street to the planes flying overhead reverberated throughout the hanger. Echoes abound, by using a floor plan, and simple formula we determine the distance sound traveled from its source there for proving the voices, and music picked up was indeed an echo from an investigator, and not evidence. By using audio spectrum analysis, we are able to determine if the voice that captured on audio was human, disembodied, or electronic voice phenomena EVP. Phenomena witnessed but was not recorded are considered observations, and are documented as personal experiences not evidence. Any observation of an unexplained nature reported immediately. Since you will never know when or where such phenomena will take place it is your ability to adapt, and change with the activity, and should be the foundation of any investigative strategy. Although experiencing such phenomenon without more than the single witness cannot be, consider reliable evidence, unless a future event supports the original claim.

Debunking seems to be a lost art these days. Everything has an explanation if you look for it. When you cannot find the explanation, you present the evidence for peer review. If it can stand up to scrutiny then it is considered evidence until proven otherwise. You must not think everything is paranormal because it is not. This is the real world, and in the real world, we look for real answers first.

While traveling we like to stay in "supposedly" haunted Hotels. It is another chance to capture activity on our trips. We routinely setup trigger objects, cameras, and voice recorders in our rooms during our stay. Just by chance, the camera in room 11 at the Gold Hill Hotel pointed at a door leading out into the hallway from the room. At 2:30 am the door to room 11 opened, and closed? Since the door did not open wide enough to see anything, or anyone, and there was no camera on the other side of the door. We threw it out as a part of our internal review process. Two years later two guests that were staying in room 11 experienced the same activity. They were standing right beside the door when it opened, and closed. They opened the door and stepped out into the hall to find no one! This shows how future evidence can support the original claim of activity.

The biggest challenge for investigators; although widely ignored are the mental disorders that account for most claims of paranormal activity. The most common are Sleep Paralysis: Awake but still asleep people often report encountering apparition-like entities or other worldly beings, Anxiety Disorders: Post-traumatic stress caused by a recent bereavement or traumatic experience, and Mental Illness: Psychotic disorders that can alter perception. I have often seen investigators prescribe metaphysical remedies in response to spiritual claims that can only end up doing more harm than good. There are unsuspected dangers when it comes to the human mind you should never take the place of a health care professional. Our memories during times of grief or illness are at their strongest. A simple act can trigger memories that can take you to a time when you envision what you expect to see, even if what you are envisioning is no longer there. Then other times it is a matter of assuming what is mistaken for what seen. It is normal for your brain to fabricate a mental representation for a substituted reality. How our brain deals with processes sensory input, comprises how we perceives the world around us, and a lot of the time that perception is wrong. We see the world around us as stable, even though our sensory input is incomplete, and rapidly changing.

Critical thinking in part based on self-correcting concepts, and principles that give consideration to standardize, and establish forms of methodology. These are fundamental in logical and plausible reasoning, and are void of assumption, or predetermined conclusions. It is important when following methods and procedures to be consistent when collecting evidence. Consistency will help ensure the evidence credibility whenever drawn into question. I have seen teams including members of my own team announce before all the evidence is gathered, analyzed, and reviewed. That they have made contact with, or have determent that! Believe you me my team knows better than to run around screaming Ghost! Do not make snap judgments, because without the preponderance of the evidence there can be no conclusion.

When investigating a location that is linked to an unsolved crime, and uncover physical evidence that might be linked to the case. Never touch potential evidence you can photograph, and document its location. Then contact local authorities, and let them decide what to do with that information. Never provide unsolicited evidence to the friends, and families of the victims. You should always turn over evidence suspected to be involved in a crime over to the proper authorities.

Control Shots, are used in part with both videography and digital photography as a process to document locations. Proper documentation can establish the precise location and relationship of objects and evidence. A control shot is a duplicate shot of a scene from which video evidence is recording, or where photographic evidence is in question. It is the purpose of documentation to record and preserve the location and relationship of discovered evidence as it was when, the documenter was observing it.

The function of scientific and technical photographers is to capture detailed and accurate photographic imagery for site documentation, and evidence reconstruction. All photographs and videography can be geo-referenced which means to establish a reference in a physical space. This enables the researcher to prepare diagrams, digitally created models, and event reconstruction. It is with the understanding that in any field of research must be taken critically before taken seriously.

Types of photography used for documenting the location. The optimal of which are 360 spherical video, 360 spherical still photographs, and high-resolution digital still photography.

Preserving the Evidence:

1. Reports and note-taking (including audio)
2. Photographs (documenting location)
3. Videography (static and mobile)
4. Floor Plans (sketching and mapping)
5. Ambient Temperature Readings
6. Accurate Measurements (static audio to reflective surfaces)

It is human nature, not all people in this world are honest, hardworking and forthcoming about their intentions. Beware of hidden agendas. I have investigated businesses that wanted to use our evidence to promote their haunt. It was only after the evidence reveal that the truth was known. They even wanted to profit off our evidence by reselling our DVD. That is why it is important to have the client sign a waiver over all rights to your work, remember your providing a service FREE. As originator of all created video by said owner under copyright law considered the work's author and the owner of its copyright, and possess the legal right to determine whether, and or how the video is used, and the participants duly releases all legal rights over all recorded materials, and by allowing you to be recorded. You release all legal rights to your image, and likeness. We had had Homeowners reporting haunts to provide them, and their friends with entertainment. Again releases, waver, confidentiality agreements. Remember contracts, and liability wavers are used to protect yourself, your members, and your property. You should always make it clear that you reserve the right to refuse service to anyone. Think of all the legalities as the price of providing a service for FREE.

If you can hear it, or see it then you can record it. The only problem is that you never know when or where it is going to occur unless you have enough equipment to cover every room. Remember human beings make very poor recorders. If you want more than personal experiences then a large investment in data, logging equipment is in order. They say a picture is worth a thousand words, but what the picture is not telling you makes a world of difference. Video tells more of a complete story, and history of events. Where a picture is a fixed point in time, and can lead everyone's mind to wander.

Chapter 7

Predisposition to fearing the Unknown

My first encounter with the paranormal occurred when I was five years old. I arrived at my grandmother and grandfather's house with my mother and sister to find my grandmother lying on the kitchen floor. My sister and I were hurried into another room as the ambulance attendants took her body away. I was too young to know or understand about death. That night, my mother, my sister, and I stayed together in a small bedroom right off the kitchen. Later that night my grandmother entered the room to check on both of us kids, as she had always done. My grandmother had watched us throughout the week while my mother worked. Therefore, it was not unusual for my grandmother to check in on us kids in that very room. I woke up and started talking with my grandmother. Though I did not see her, I felt her presence, and knew she was sitting at the foot of the bed. Lying next to me, my mother awakened when she heard me talking. As soon as my mother realized whom I was talking too, she yelled out, 'Oh, my God, my mother is in the room!' As my mother screamed, I saw the black shape of my grandma stand up, and leave the room. I did not understand what happened, or why my mother was so upset. When I spoke with my grandmother, I did not feel afraid or threatened in anyway in fact it was a calming, and reassuring experience. Throughout my childhood and early teenage years, I would stay up all night watching the late-night creature features on television. They taught me to be afraid of whatever goes bump in the night. As a paranormal researcher, I still am caught up in the creepiness of the moment at some of the locations. The winery investigation that our team attended could have been taken right out of an old horror movie, even to details such as the howling dogs and the thick foggy nights. However, I have long since realized that there is nothing to fear. The underlying question is what is reality, when reports of being touched, shoved, or hearing a disembodied voice telling you to leave. Research shows that it is normal for us to create a subjective reality when placed alone in the dark, but there is so much more that has not been so easily explained away.

My second encounter with the paranormal occurred in the summer of 2005. I worked night shift, so I slept all morning upstairs. Some times during the day, the temperature would reach over 112 degrees, which made it impossible to sleep. Therefore, I started sleeping downstairs in the guest bedroom. After I bought, the house a next-door neighbor told me that a young handicapped girl died in that room from cancer. No one has ever stayed in that room, and at that time, I was not involved in anything paranormal. I never had any problems sleeping there during the day. Until one night, I had the night off; I was so exhausted that I did not have the energy to walk upstairs to bed, so I slept in the guest room. I just walked in, and fell face down toward the foot of the bed. At 3 o'clock in the morning, I felt someone pull the hair out from the front of my head. I immediately looked up to see a small hand, and arm slide down between the footboard and the mattress. My immediate thought was 'Okay now it is under the bed!' I stared at the gap between the footboard and the mattress, and waited until morning when I could see the room clearly. I got out of bed, and walked into the bathroom in the hallway. Looking in the mirror, I could see where my hair had been pulled out. Later in the afternoon, I checked the bed. There I found hair on the edge of the mattress, and all the way down under the bed. That is when I first started asking questions about life after death, and I have continued asking those questions for the past seven years realizing that there may be a very real possibility of an afterlife.

My third encounter with the paranormal occurred when my wife's father passed away in 2010. I did not know him all that well but he knew I hunted ghosts. Those weeks after the funeral my wife stayed with her sisters, I returned home every night. I would hear three knocks on the window by the bed, then again on the back door of the bedroom that led outside. Every night I would get up and look to see nothing. I would hear that knocking all night long. Went out the back door repeatedly too find nothing! A couple days of continuous activity always, the same three knocks something unique happened. While lying in bed I felt something around my toes on my left foot. I kept looking down at the end of the bed at my foot. It felt warm around my toes as if someone had cupped their hands around it. Then suddenly the foot moved off the bed! I responded with thank you, do it again! Ghost Hunter Response! Later when my wife returned home, I told her I keep hearing a knock on the back door only to find nothing. She told me when her father came over to the house he would knock three times. Something I did not know, but after my foot, being pulled off the bed I figured something was going on. I eventually told her that it was three knocks that I was hearing on the door, but never told her about my foot. Soon after my foot was pulled off the bed, the activity ended. My needing to know what was real and what is explainable took on new meaning, and even though I researched the paranormal, I was never sure that what I was experiencing was a hallucination or parasomnia. I questioned EVPs can I find a way to validate what is real, from fantasy you find so much in the paranormal field.

Is it a Ghost Story?

There are challenges that lie before us

There is no proof that any of these experiences ever happen. People want to believe so badly that they will accept any story even if it is full of inaccuracies or half-truths entirely on face value. In the paranormal field, everyone has a really good ghost story.

Extracting fact from fiction comes down to procedures and documentation. This is the reason behind the two-interview process. The report of activity filed then followed up with a phone interview. This to determine the accuracy, and resolve of the applicant. If the applicant is serious about what has been experienced. The walk-through is scheduled with our new client. After arriving, the second interview process begins in addition to the drawing of floor plans. Control photographs are taken of the area. A review of the recorded audio along with all the data collected will determine the accuracy of the claim submitted. This is how you can determine if you are there to help the client, or provide them with the night's entertainment.

Agendas run deep

Then there is the hidden agenda this is never clearly apparent until after the investigation starts. We have had clients dictating an investigation strategy from watching Para-non-reality TV shows. One client told me to shut off the lights because the ghosts do not like them on. I explained that there are case studies conducted at University College London that said when a group of people placed in a dark, silent room, many start hallucinating after just a few minutes, and that probably explains most of those shows. We have showed up to homes the night of the investigation filled with family, and friends wanting to be a part of the night's entertainment, more than once. We had to make it perfectly clear that only the homeowner was allowed there all night with us. When this happens, it is best to draw a line they leave or you leave. You cannot capture clear or valid responses when there is that much contamination you might as well go home. This had gotten so bad that we added a letter to the forms we give the client explaining paranormal shows to clarify what their expectations are from us.

LETTER: The Reality of Paranormal Reality Shows

People that have seen shows like Ghost Hunters, and Ghost Adventures do not realize that filming a forty-minute show where it looks like they investigated overnight, in reality took a film crew following your favorite investigator around on location an average of ten days. They stay in wardrobe wearing identical clothing during the filming, so in editing they match throughout the show.

Real paranormal investigations are usually limited to 4, or five hours over the duration of a single night. Rarely are we ever allowed to investigate a location longer than one night. Regardless of how much we would want too! We are very thorough in our analysis of the evidence. Even though capturing activity of any kind since we never know when or where it may occur is rare. Then again, there have been investigations that produced no activity at all or very subtle activity during the length of the investigation.

We want you to know that activity you may have seen on reality paranormal shows are not entirely real, and the quality of the activity during the single night can change in intensity in the days to come. If the activity you are experiencing was not real. We would not be doing the research, and you would not be inviting us into your home. We wanted to make sure that your expectations are not based on what you may have seen on some paranormal reality TV show.

Chapter 8

Convincing Evidence of an Afterlife
(Articulatory Phonetics)

The Fourier transform method is at the core of modern signal processing and analysis, and is the science behind Articulatory Phonetics and the physics of sound. Fourier analysis series used in applied mathematics, and gets its name from a French mathematician and physicist named Jean Baptiste Joseph (Baron) de Fourier.

The Fourier transform is one of the specific forms of Fourier analysis, and essential to understanding more complex wave structures, like human speech. Given a complicated, messy wave function like a recording of a person talking, the Fourier transform allows us to break the messy function into a combination of a number of simple waves, greatly simplifying analysis. When processing signals, such as audio, radio waves, light waves, seismic waves, and even images, Fourier analysis can isolate individual components of a compound waveform, concentrating them for easier detection and/or removal. A large family of signal processing techniques consist of Fourier-transforming a signal, manipulating the Fourier-transformed data in a simple way, and reversing the transformation.

Articulatory Phonetics is the study of the sound waves produced by human speech, and is the key to understanding a valid EVP response. I have developed methods, and procedures with the purpose of collecting data that can easily evaluated professionally. Along with the use of Spectrum Analysis an advanced mathematical technique for the study of frequencies according to its component wavelengths producing a visual representation, call a spectrogram, or (sonogram). Primarily used in astronomy, music, signal research, and electronics.

I will provide just enough basic information to familiarize you with basic articulatory phonetics, and the phonology of North American English, phonemes and basic contrasts without getting into major allophonic variation such as vowel nasalization, and nasal place assimilation.

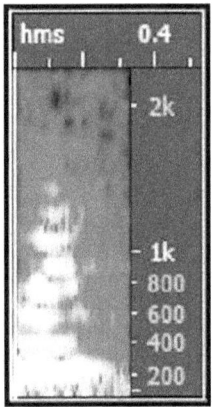

A formant is a dark band shown here in yellow for Color, or white in the B&W addition in a wide band spectrogram, which corresponds to a vocal tract resonance. In speech, primarily the vibration of the vocal folds provides the source of sound.

Spacing between the harmonic changes up, or down with the pitch of the voice.

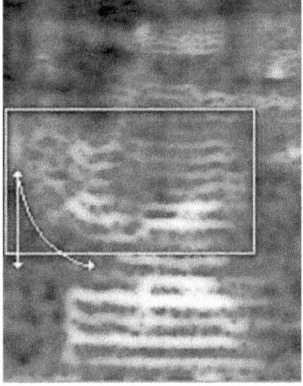

Technically, it represents a set of adjacent harmonics, which boosted by a resonance in some part of the vocal tract. Thus, different vocal tract shapes will produce different formant patterns, regardless of what the source is doing. There's the turbulence generated by the air as it moves past the walls of the vocal tract, usually called 'channel frication'. This is just 'drag', resistance to the free flow of air. Frication noises are generated in two ways, either by blowing air against an object 'obstacle frication' or moving air through a narrow channel into a relatively more open space 'channel frication'.

Voicing represented on a wide band spectrogram by vertical striations, especially in the lowest frequencies. Each vertical 'line' represents a single pulse of the vocal folds, a single puff of air moving through the glottis.

Frication noise is generated in two ways, by either blowing air against an object (obstacle frication) or moving air through a narrow channel into a relatively more open space (channel frication).

Plosives refer to voice less sound from produced by complete closure of the oral passage and subsequent release accompanied by a burst of air.

Nasals (Nasal stops) have some formant structure, but are better identified in lower amplitude than in the vowel. Best described as a resonance left over in the nasal tract.

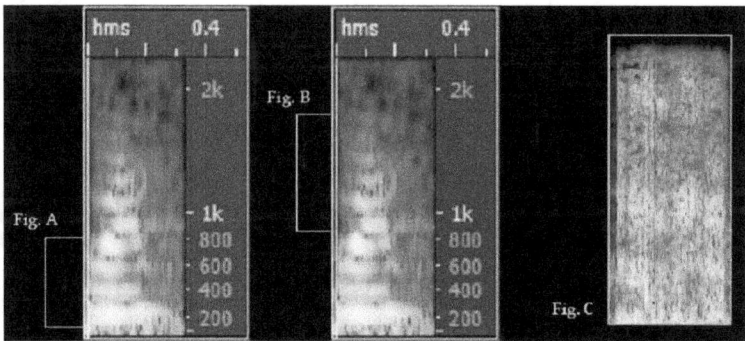

Noise is random (rather than striated or harmonically organized) energy. (Fig. C)

The first formant correlates to height (openness) of the vocal tract. The formant with the lowest frequency called f1, the second f2, and the third f3. (Fig. A)

The next highest formant in the vowel space correlates vowel quality, and vowel duration. Vowels will usually have four or more distinguishable formants; sometimes there are more than six. The first two formants are enough to determine vowel quality.

The final burst is the release of the final plosive, and the last bit of noise echoing around the vocal tract. In a wide band spectrogram as weaker formants and turbulence generated by the air as it moves past the walls of the vocal tract called channel frication. If you want to know, more take a class in acoustic phonetics. (Fig. B)

When comparing human speech to the response from the anomaly. You can clearly see vowels in human speech will usually have four or more distinguishable formants followed by vertical striations caused by air movement through the glottis to drive vibration. It is the lack of these characteristics such as vibration of the vocal folds. That distinguishes human speech from a valid electronic voice response. In the entities response there is no physical signs of a throat, mouth, or breath. Remember you must understand there are numerous skeptical explanations all them are true when it comes to the inexperienced paranormal team. For a professional organization to be taken seriously you needs to address every skeptical concern, and there is no shortage of skeptical concerns.

Convincing Evidence of an Afterlife

(EVP Frequency Analysis)

Electronic Voice Phenomena commonly known as an EVP among ghost-hunting enthusiasts. Others and I agree that there are more than one attribute that is associated with the phenomenon, so a more accurate description would be Anomalous Voice Phenomena, AVP.

There is an extensive history of the phenomenon with many notable physicists, and Universities dating to the original discovery back in 1949, the technology of the time, the first reel-to-reel tape recorder called a Magnetophon.

In 1965 Dr. Konstantīns Raudive worked with Friedrich Jürgenson to make what was then called EVP recordings. Later with the help of various electronics experts from Pye Records, and physicists from AT&T recorded over 100,000 audiotapes, most of which were made under what he described as "strict laboratory conditions." Over 400 people were involved in his research, and all apparently heard the voices. This culminated in the 1968 publication of Unhörbares wird hörbar "What is inaudible becomes audible" published in English in 1971 as Breakthrough. The following year, more controlled experiments took place. English company Belling and Lee, Ltd., used by the British government to test its most sophisticated defense equipment, decided to conduct some experiments with Raudive at their Radio-Frequency-Screened Laboratory. The supervising engineer, Peter Hale, was a physicist and electronics engineer. He was considered the leading expert on electronic-suppression in Great Britain, and one of the five leading sound engineers in the West. The recording hardware which was designed for this test was provided, and the blank tape which had just been shipped from the factory was used. But the voices still appeared.

A.P, Hale stated:
In view of the tests carried out in a screened laboratory at my firm, I cannot explain what happened in normal physical terms. Raudive continued researching such alleged voices on his own and spent much of the last ten years of his life exploring EVP.

Technology has come along way since the late 1970s, and early 80s the nearest thing to a portable computer called an Osborne also called a "luggable", the Marketing Department called it a "hernia". The understanding of the phenomena and it's detractors have explained away a large part of "why it can't be." I can't emphasize enough that most EVPs are explainable. Especially when it involves the inexperienced, and uneducated.

Skeptical Explanations for EVP:

1. Noise Contamination
2. RF Contamination
3. Human Speech Mistaken for an EVP
4. Stomach Noise
5. Breath
6. Echo

Collecting data correctly requires rigorous disciplines something the ghost-hunting enthusiast is not willing to do. Simply put they are just not in it for the data, or the real work that is involved. I have had members in my own team mentioned that doing research "the correct way" took the fun out of the paranormal. When the primary focus is scaring one another in the dark, or bolstering evidence that in the real world means nothing at all. I have yet seen anyone in the paranormal community that has the slightest clue on how to preserve the integrity of the data.

How voice recorders can record what our ears cannot hear. The average frequency ranges on these audio devises are between 40Hz – 21,000 Hz well within the range of human hearing of 20Hz – 20,000 Hz, Electronic Voice Phenomena described as being within the bandwidth of 60Hz to 28Hz. On a wideband spectrogram within the range of 800Hz to 4 kHz, it is not so much that it is above or below the range of human hearing just that the amplitude is too faint to be heard by the human ear. When the volume played back, it is turn all the way up the same goes for audio editors. We found it necessary to use headphone amplifiers in aiding us in identifying the voice anomalies, audio spectrum analysis, and procedures developed along with training to ask questions that would require an extended answer at the point where we would be listening for the response. An extensive understanding, and comprehensive knowledge of Acoustic and Articulatory Phonetics are requires in separating the differences between noise and human speech patterns from the artificial characteristics of a true AVP. The experiments we have conducted show that the anomaly exists well within our physical plain of existence.

Addressing EVP Skeptical Arguments
You must understand this is just a beginning there are numerous skeptical explanations all them are true when it comes to the inexperienced paranormal team. For a professional organization to be taken seriously you needs to address every skeptical concern, and there is no shortage of skeptical concerns.

1, 4, 5. Noise Contamination, Stomach Noise, Breathing
Being able to show documented procedures and methods of research will answer most but not all of them.

Such as an EVP procedure, outlining relaxed breathing techniques, and learning to hold your breath for 15 seconds after asking the question.

Controlling stomach noise by drinking, plenty of warm water or any other warm drinks even 7-up will work; this will line your stomach. Snacks you could eat a cracker or a piece of bread, and burping when appropriate.

Having written procedures is another way to validate the audio, rotating small groups limiting the number of people at the location.

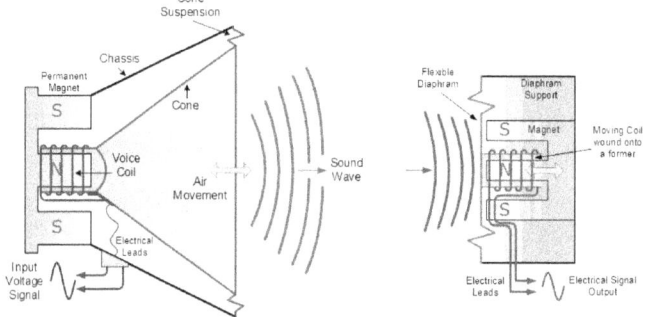

2. RF Contamination

Let us first understand how a microphone can pick up an EM response. The dynamic microphones' design is very simple there is a cone that attached to a magnet surrounded by a coil of wire. When the cone picks up sound, it vibrates moving the attached magnet up, and down in the coil creating a current through the wire. Now the speaker is simply the same device but backwards. The current moves through the coil causing the magnet attached to the cone to move the cone up and down reproducing sound. The EM field would act upon the coil in the microphone instead of an acoustical response that would act on the cone.

This is the idea behind the coil microphone I built to record RF contamination. It is a coil or RF choke, wire wrapped around a ferrite core to enhance the electronic signal then plugged into a voice recorder to record any RF contamination during the AVP session. This easily built specialize device that is sensitive enough to record electromagnetic fields to an audio recorder that can produce a spectrogram showing any electromagnetic contamination before, during, and after the time of the audios creation, and would address RF contamination.

I wanted to see what a Radio broadcast looked like recorded from a Radio receiver bypassing the speaker recorded directly into the audio recorder. The reason why I am bypassing the speaker is to simulate contamination from the broadcast through the coil built into the dynamic microphone of the audio recorder.

What I am looking for are patterns of human speech with nonhuman characteristics from RF contamination.

This was actually easy to do with a speaker-less Radio Shack Radio and a stereo male-to-male patch cable into the audio recorder. What I got was visible human speech, and a lot of station noise shown here.

Testing Artificial Speech:
An artificial voice like a text to speech program has the same characteristics as human speech because how the simulated voice enunciates words. Vowels in the words would create the same formant structure you see in human speech. What you do not see is vibration as air moves through the glottis unless played through a speaker. Then the vibrating speaker would simulate the sound of vibration or air movement.

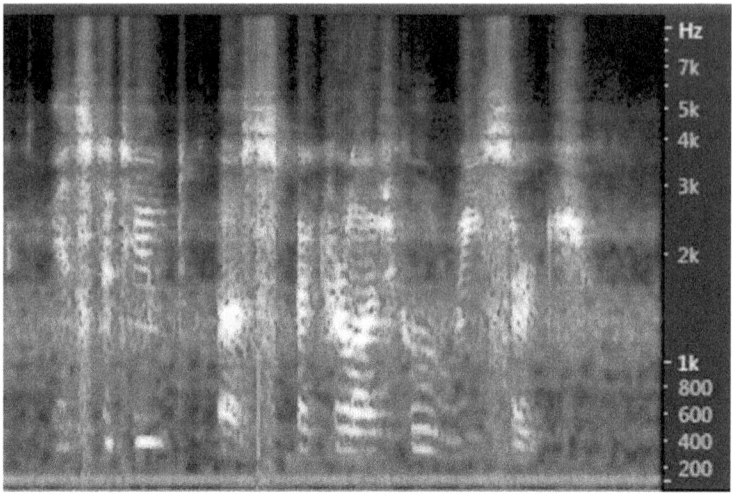

There is one other possibility and that is human speech at a distance. We all know voices can carry from within the location, and from outside. Distance can severely reduce the clarity of human speech. I recorded the same human voice with two audio recorders at varying distances from 10 to 25 feet, and what I found was some similarities to EVPs. It is still similar enough to human speech with a good imagination you might be able to create something out of it, 'Audio Pareidolia'. To most novus groups this would be an easy mistake then again any noise recorded from a distance could be mistaken for an EVP. In a spectrogram the formant structure, flatten down to long wavy lines. The greater the distance the less unintelligible the sound becomes as speech. This is just another way to show what "speech like sounds" look like that picked up by the audio recorder. There is no example of speech human or otherwise that can compare with the audio recorded from the anomaly we picked up an undisclosed location.

3. Human Speech Mistaken for an EVP

When comparing human speech to the response from the entity. You can clearly see vowels in human speech will usually have four or more distinguishable formants followed by vertical striations caused by air movement through the glottis to drive vibration. It is the lack of these characteristics such as vibration of the vocal folds. That distinguishes human speech from a valid anomalous voice response. In the entities response there is no physical signs of a throat, mouth, or breath.

A blind Physicist David Kent Cullers joined us on a couple investigations. I had an idea on how I could explain human speech in a formant structure when referring to a valid AVP response in an audio spectrogram. Picture in your mind a 6-foot stepladder. The shorter ladders are wider at the bottom, and narrower at the top. The ladder has rungs, or steps separated by space. The formants in a spectrogram for human speech look like a ladder, but at differing widths depending on the length of the word pronounced. The lower or bottom three to six steps are vowels they are mirrored above by three to six steps, but weaker, and shorter as they move up the ladder. This is friction as air moves through the glottis over the tongue through the teeth and the lips, or through the nose. Above that is a uniformed pattern that moves all the way up the spectrogram created by airflow. A valid electronic voice response has one-step maybe another shorter second step, but no friction or vertical uniformed pattern created by airflow. Therefore, we are saying that it has no mouth or breath.

Document who is on each team limiting each team to two or three researchers. Have audio samples of each member from holding the audio recorder then 3 feet from the recorder to 6 feet, and 15 feet away because human speech that looks like a ladder in an audio spectrogram near the recorder starts to collapse down to a couple long lines the farther away from the audio recorder you are. Remember, validating audio with the use of audio spectrum analysis, and educating yourself on Articulatory Phonetics: the spectrological study of human speech.

6. Echo:

In the example of an echo, the frequency reduces as it reverberates, dropping lower in the spectrogram. One very notable observation when the frequency reduces in human speech the formant structure collapses dropping lower and lower. The more distant the sound source is from the audio recorder the lower the frequencies causing the formant structure in human speech to collapse into one or two lines at the bottom of the spectrogram. The quality of speech at the lower frequencies are indiscernible as speech being realistic of what comprises the phonology of any particular language. As formant, structures collapse the AVP show up as one or two short events high up in the spectrogram from 800Hz-4kHz at a bandwidth between 28Hz-38Hz higher amplitude AVP above 60Hz move into another category known as the disembodied voice.

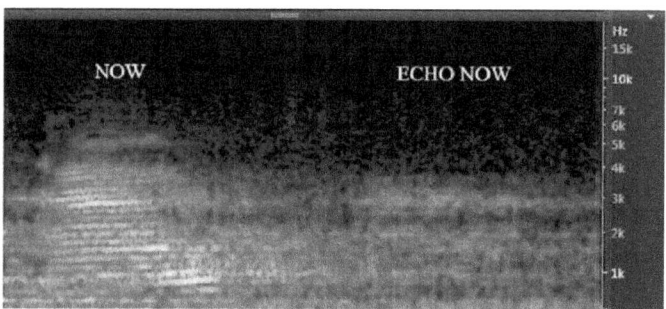

Echo vs. Reverberation

A reverberation is reflected sound waves combine with your original sound waves, both characteristics of the echo, and reverberation as described has no resemblance to responses recorded from questions asked. These responses are well-documented observations. The problem with an echo, or reverberation as an explanation for electronic voice phenomena would not explain why most responses carry specific meaning attributed to the researcher. I have seen echo phenomena mistaken for responses from only the most inexperienced of paranormal teams. Document throughout the location and in each area the ambient temperature. This is another way to answer yet another skeptical explanation. Used together with floor plans measure the distance from static audio devices to the nearest reflective surfaces can help validate the audio as other than an echo.

Remember you need to address every skeptical explanation on why your data should be taken seriously.

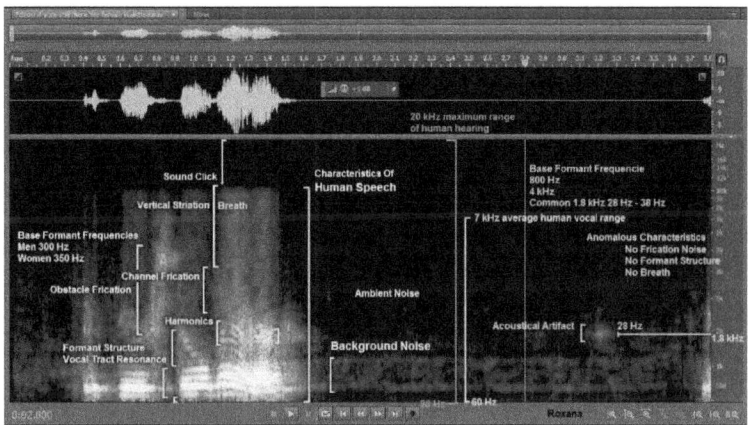

I have been comparing frequencies of reoccurring clear electronic voice phenomenon from the same anomaly repeating the same word, each time the same word repeated at the same frequency. This could suggest that the anomaly has a unique frequency fingerprint for certain words. The word was her name Roxanna, each time recorded on different days, and at different times.

Altering low frequency responses by simply changing the pitch of any noise by slowing it down, or speeding it up can manipulate the sound to come up with whatever you might think it said, or want it to say. The idea is to control your environment, tag your audio; backing up your audio with video can help validate responses, use audio spectrum analysis to rule out questionable sounds that could be mistaken for evidence. The more control you have over the environment the less time spent on audio analysis. We use Adobe Audition audio editing software that will allow you to remove noise from around the sound you want to bring out for use on videos. If the EM response intended as evidence is not clear enough that everyone without help, guessing, or manipulating the sound, can understand it. Throw it out!

There is a University Study published in Sept. 2012 of a series of experiments carried out in Vigo, Spain. Throughout a period of two years under conditions controlled to the highest degree achievable entitled: "A Two-Year Investigation of the Allegedly Anomalous Electronic Voices or EVP" by Corresponding author: Anabela Cardoso they outlined some of the problems they've had with stomach noises, whispering, sound being mistaken for voices, and contamination. Addressing the contamination problem with new procedures, the same methods we have already adopted to address skeptical explanations for anomalous voice phenomena-AVP what others call an EVP. Their conclusion in this study was that the data was real, and yet unexplained.

I encourage everyone to read this research, everything we had already discovered, and addressed with changes in procedures, training, and methodology. Learning to relax your breathing, drinking plenty of warm fluids, and practicing speaking at a moderate tone between 50-60 dB with the use of a decibel meter, no yelling out your AVP questions their dead not deaf, and no whispering ever.

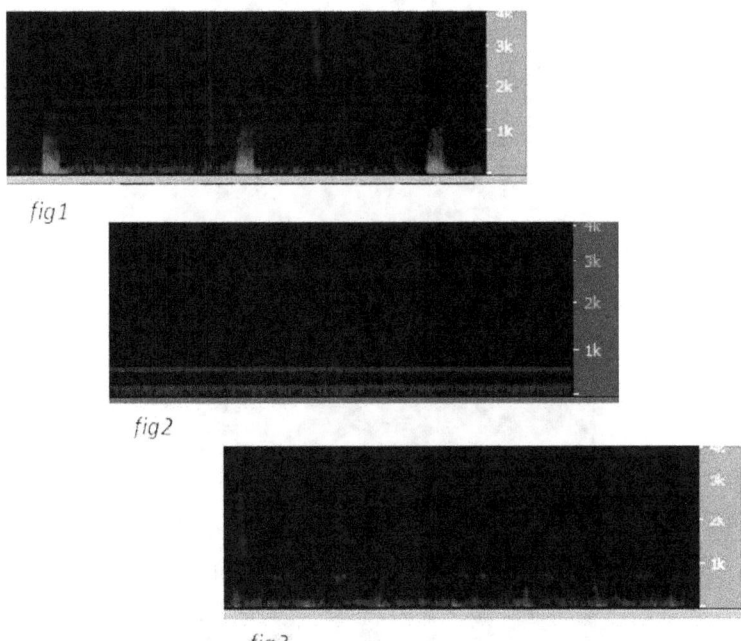

fig1

fig2

fig3

In sampling Radio Frequency and RF contamination from different locations, we investigated. *(Shown above)*
fig1. Home security system
fig2. Residence in Stockton
fig3. Oakland Airport Museum

What I am seeing from *fig2-3* is multiple bands of continuous noise the only differences is *fig1* the home security system that shows a continuous pulsed. I wanted to see what a Radio broadcast looked like recorded from a Radio receiver bypassing the speaker recorded directly into the audio recorder.

The next couple of pages contain more examples of sound.

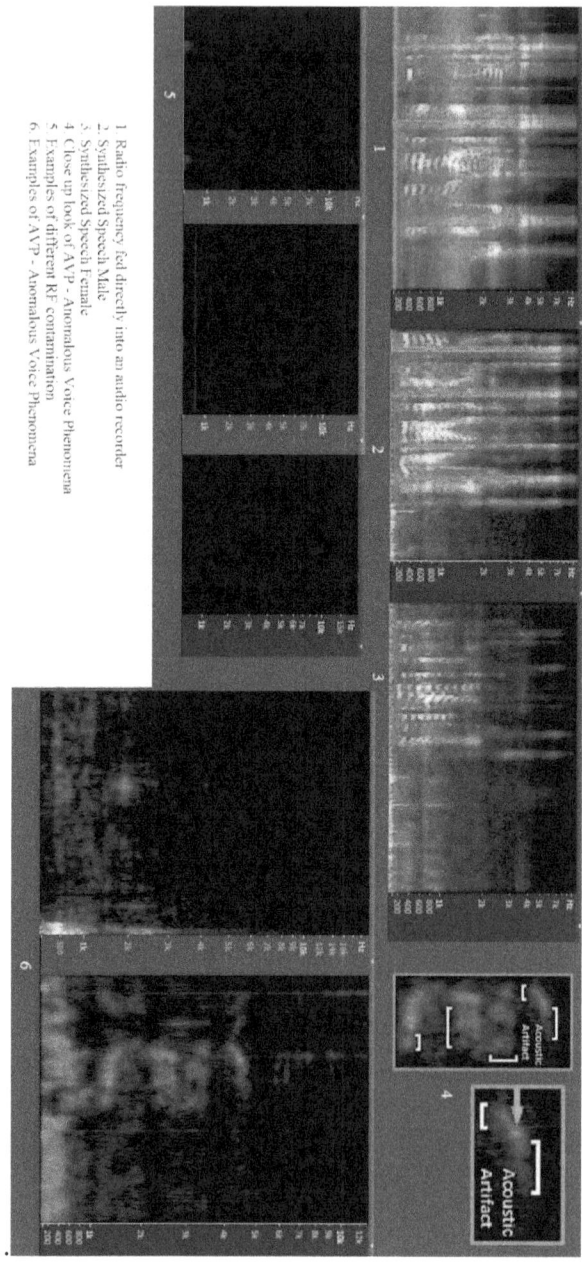

1 Radio frequency fed directly into an audio recorder
2 Synthesized Speech Male
3 Synthesized Speech Female
4 Close up look of AVP - Anomalous Voice Phenomena
5 Examples of different RF contamination
6 Examples of AVP - Anomalous Voice Phenomena

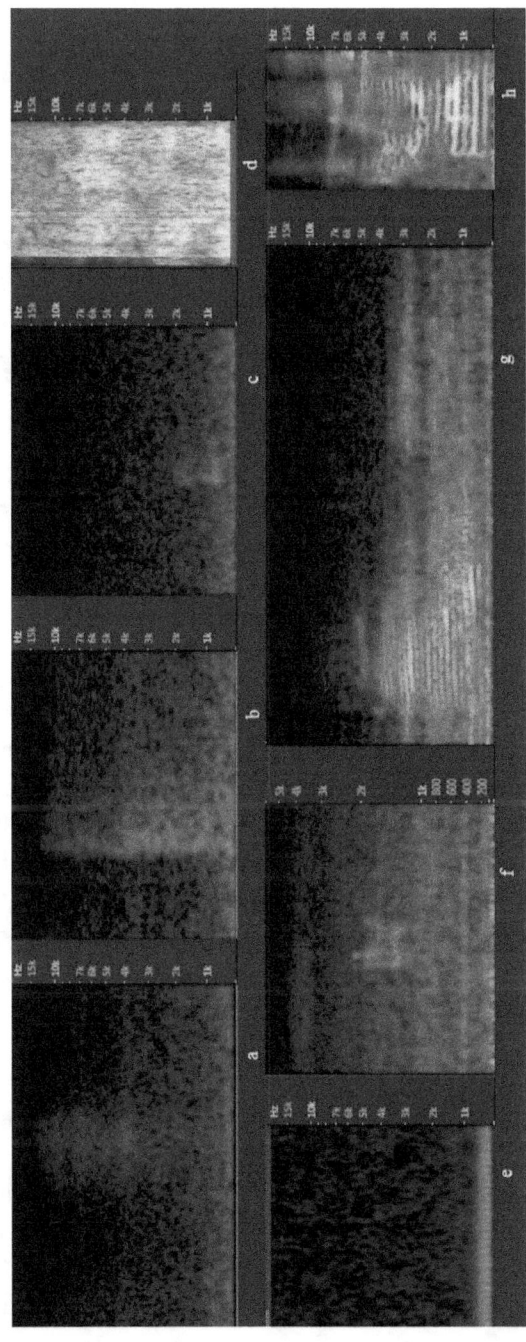

a. Breath
b. House Settling noise (POP)
c. Knock

d. Dragging Noise
e. Stomach Noise
f. Throat Noise

g. Echo Human Speech
h. Human Speech

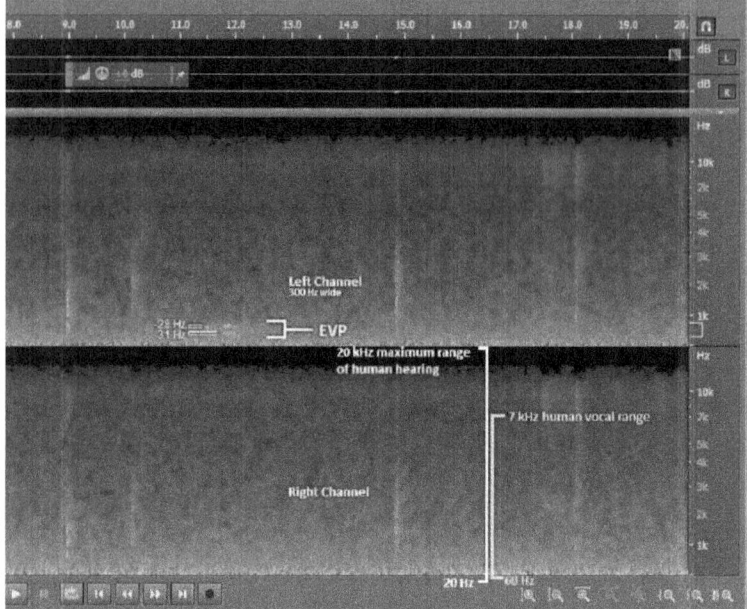

Targeting

One of the audio anomalies we have encountered are the many examples of targeting. To gain a better understanding of what is actually happening I tested Olympus 600/700 audio recorders with and without external Sony ECM-DS70P Electret Condenser microphones, showing the anomaly can target its acoustical voice, shown above in the spectrogram. The reason for using external microphones is to reduce noise contamination through the embedded microphones in the body of the recorder.

Condenser microphones consist of a capacitor with one plate fixed and the other forming the diaphragm moved by sound waves. The inductance of the capacitor's wire leads is susceptible to RF interference. Although not as much as the dynamic microphone which is far more sensitive to RF contamination. We also tested the imitation Sony ECM-

DS70P and found them to have a better high frequency response.

When laying out voice recorders in circles, end to end, side to side, directly in front of the researchers. Using both dynamic, and condenser microphones we found the anomaly could target its response. In one experiment when we looked at the audio from the Zoom 360 4-channel microphones it showed a linear path across the room to the researchers' recorder. We position team members around a table with their recorders directly in front of them showing targeted responses.

Another explanation of targeting described to me by using sound reflection. That sound waves bounce around the room reflecting off the surfaces in the room. Different surfaces absorb frequencies differently, so that some audio recorders would record the sound while others would not depending on location, and the materials nearest the audio device. The sound engineer's explanation is valid for frequencies of 30dB and higher, but has not taken into account the amplitude of frequencies below -44dB there is a cost of absorption loss when reflecting sound waves at low amplitude would quickly reduce the frequency to zero, supporting a line of sight, other than reflection.

Having an explanation does not necessarily mean there is an absolute conclusion.

A simpler explanation to explain the targeting results for stereo microphones would be a channel failure along with sound reflection if it were not for multiple incidences using different audio recorders. I guess if the answer were easy, we would not call it an anomaly.

The difference between an electronic voice phenomena and a disembodied voice is the amplitude of the sound wave.

There is a frequency threshold between electromagnetic voice phenomena and acoustical artifact in an anomalous voice response. Which would also explain the results between the dynamic or condenser microphone it's not so much as being vulnerable to EM frequencies as to which is better at picking up faint low-frequency sound.

If your focus is to bring science into your explanation. Even if you had extraordinary data, simply using the wrong wording in your description, understanding that links to terminology outside the framework of science will label your work as completely ridiculous and foolhardy. New data explaining new phenomenon needs new terminology that are unique to your discovery.

Convincing Evidence of an Afterlife
(More Questions than Answers)

Analyzing one of our intelligent responses caught on audio, we called Anomalous Voice Phenomena - AVP. The audio when we listened to it exhibited so much diversity in its response. In both cognitive, and physical traits that are only found in living human beings. The most remarkable is precognition that we thought was impossible without a physical presence. Then there is the absence of sensory organs, which would be necessary to accomplice such a physiological process. The anomaly first displayed the ability to _see_ the actions taken by the researcher as the attempt was made to open a locked dresser drawer. The capacity to comprehend, and yet display precognition is the foundation of human consciousness, and our higher cognitive abilities. This is firmly established within its first _spoken_ response. '*It's Locked*' the anomaly again displays comprehension and the ability to _hear_ as the researcher acknowledges the locked drawer by responding with a confirmation, and an emotional expletive. The anomaly responded with '*It is, Fuck You!*' Not one single physical region of the human brain could explain the complexity of this response. To date there is no proof that our brain can survive physical death, so the explanation must lie within the yet undiscovered properties of the brain.

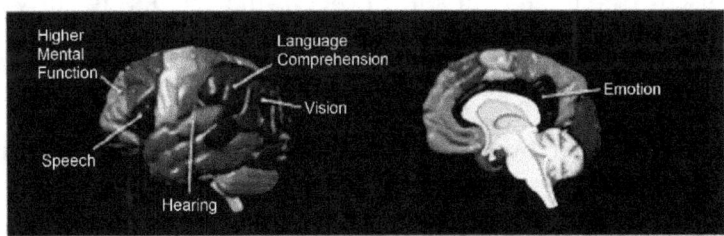

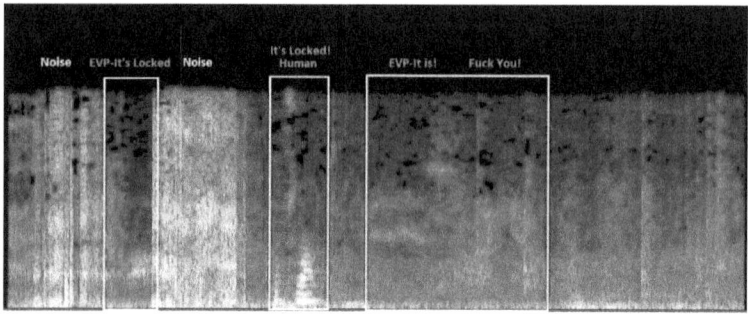

When comparing the formant between this EVP, and Human speech in a wide band spectrogram. The formant in the EVP shows no vertical striations.

The female response of the acknowledgment 'It's locked'. The first word 'Its' shows three clear formants with vertical striations comprised of one formant obstacle frication.

In the second word of the female response 'locked' shows six clear formants with vertical striations comprised of three-formant obstacle frication.

The obstacle frication in the vertical striations signify obstructions caused by air movement through the vocal cords, tongue, teeth, and lips unlike the entities response that shows no vertical striations or obstacle frication.

Vowels in human speech will usually have four or more distinguishable formants followed by vertical striations caused by air movement through the glottis to drive vibration. Again, the EVP shows no vertical striations.

It is the lack of these characteristics such as vibration of the vocal folds. That distinguishes human speech from a valid electronic voice response

One more piece of evidence I wanted to point out. The room they were in was 20x15x15 foot (6.1x4.6x4.6 meters) was full of large pieces of furniture the observation would have had to been made just behind the left shoulder of the researcher. Again female speech shows formant structure the anomaly none.

It's locked (It's Locked) it is Fuck You

Soundcloud snd.sc/10hDvHI

In order to hear the low amplitude responses clearly you may need to turn up the volume, or put on headphones.

There are single blind, and double blind studies the difference is when certain knowledge withheld from the interviewer and interviewee to obtain subjective non-bias results that are preexisting in the mind. The single blind study the interviewer the researcher knew the origin of the voices that were listened too. The interviewee was asked what could be heard to what was heard while other researchers noted people's reactions.

Voice Recognition Study

Conducted single blind study of the audio **'It's Locked'** the evaluators listen to the audio and asked what they heard.

One hundred people surveyed on Saturday October (6, 13, 20, 27) 2012 from (9am-10pm) at Dell-Osso Farms Lathrop, California

EVP response 'it's locked'
80% missed the first EVP response due to the noise as the researcher tried to open a locked drawer.
20% did not know
80% heard 'it's locked' after isolating EVP response from noise.

Female response of 'it's locked'
100% heard 'it's locked'

EVP response 'it is'
60% heard 'it is'
10% did not know
30% heard voice

EVP responses 'fuck you'
100% heard 'fuck you'

Equipment Used
Two laptops Dell/HP, 6 Sony standard headphones, 3 headphone Radio Shack amplifiers called 'boostaroo'.

A new audio anomalies study is conducted every year throughout the month of October at Dell-Osso Farms Lathrop, California.

Chapter 9

Brief History of Electronic Voice Phenomena - EVP

Thomas Edison was asked in a 1920 interview published in the Scientific American.

"If our personality survives, then it is strictly logical and scientific to assume that it retains memory, intellect, and other faculties and knowledge that we acquire on earth..."

"...I am inclined to believe that our personality hereafter will be able to affect matter. If this reasoning be correct, then, if we can evolve an instrument so delicate as to be affected, moved, or manipulated...by our personality as it survives in the next life, such an instrument, when made available, ought to record something."

An American photographer Attila von Szalay was among the first to try recording what he believed to be voices of the dead. He began his attempts in 1941 using a 78-rpm record, but it was not until 1956, after switching to a microphone and reel-to-reel tape recorder that Attila von Szalay along with Raymond Bayless believed they were successful. Von Szalay and Bayless' work published by the Journal of the American Society for Psychical Research in 1959. Bayless later went on to co-author the 1979 book, 'Phone Calls from the Dead.'

In 1959, Swedish painter and film producer Friedrich Jürgenson was recording bird songs. Upon playing the tape later, he heard what he interpreted to be his dead father's voice and then the spirit of his deceased wife calling his name. He went on to make several more recordings, including one that he said contained a message from his late mother.

In 1964, Dr. Konstantin Raudive, a student of Carl Jung, a Latvian psychologist who taught at the University Of Uppsala, Sweden read Friedrich Jürgenson's book, Voices from Space, and impressed by it that he arranged to meet Jürgenson in 1965. Raudive asked Jürgenson to demonstrate some of his tapes to a small private audience. Since the demonstration was successful, Raudive started some research with Jürgenson on his estate in order to gain some personal experience. Raudive started researching such alleged voices on his own and spent much of the last ten years of his life exploring EVP. With the help of various electronics experts, he recorded over 100,000 audiotapes, most of which were made under what he described as "strict laboratory conditions." He collaborated at times with Bender. Over 400 people were involved in his research, and all apparently heard the voices. This culminated in the 1968 publication of Unhörbares wird hörbar.

In 1971, Pye Records Ltd. invited Raudive to their sound lab and installed special equipment to block out any radio and television signals, which they could detect at that time. They would not allow Raudive to touch any of the equipment. Raudive used one tape recorder, which was monitored by a control tape recorder. All he could do was speak into a microphone. They taped Raudive's voice for eighteen minutes and none of the experimenters heard any other sounds. Nevertheless, when the scientists played back the tape, to their amazement, they heard over two hundred voices on it. Observers accepted the validity of EVP since some voices addressed Raudive as his nickname, "Kosti" or "Koste," and Raudive's deceased sister said her name three times "Tekle."

Revisiting on how later recordings were conducted within the screened chamber at a laboratory with all the shielding from radio frequencies. When the common assumption over the years, that the properties of the anomaly are electromagnetic. How then were they able to record two hundred voices? It would be self-defeating since the screening would ground any electromagnetic source unless our understanding of both the entities properties and electronic voice phenomenon are wrong, or the screening may have been adequate for the time, but inadequate in blocking all EM frequencies.

Consequently, English edition of the book "Breakthrough" published. In the next year, more controlled experiment was took place. The English company Belling and Lee, Ltd., used by the British government to test its most sophisticated defense equipment, decided to conduct some experiments with Raudive at their Radio-Frequency-Screened Laboratory. The supervising engineer, Peter Hale, was a physicist and electronics engineer. He considered the leading expert on electronic-suppression in Great Britain, and one of the five leading sound engineers in the West. The recording hardware that designed for this test was provided, and the blank tape that had just been shipped from the factory was used. Nevertheless, the voices still appeared.

A.P. Hale, Physicist and Electronics Engineer stated:
In view of the tests carried out in a screened laboratory at my firm, I cannot explain what happened in normal physical terms.

University Study published in September 2012 conducted in Vigo, Spain throughout a period of two years testing of the allegedly anomalous electronic voices, or EVP, under controlled acoustic conditions.

"The voice was captured by both the dynamic and the condenser microphones and although, as usual, the recording levels were set at the same value for both microphones, the Shure SM 58 recording is much lower (the utterance has peak amplitude of -41,6dB). As happened throughout the experiments, although lower, the sound seems to be more defined in the dynamic micro file than in the condenser file with a peak of -19,5 dB (Files SM 58_05 and U 87_03, minute 07':20''). This is most likely due to the characteristics of the microphones."

"Since the time of Jürgenson's and Raudive's experiments, there have been an increasing number of reports from all over the world of people who claim to receive the voices of the deceased through electronic means. While a good number of those reports might be attributed to pareidolia, there are others, which deserve attention and should be carefully examined since the reported communications seem to carry the meaning attributed to them by the operator and other listeners."

(Brune, 2005; 2006; Brune and Chauvin, 1999; Cardoso, ibid 2010; Cardoso, CD, 2010; Locher and Harsch, 1989; Senkowski, 1989; 1995)

Chapter 10

Animals in the Paranormal (Animal Haunts)

"Rudolf Steiner believed animal consciousness to be the experience of desires, hopes and fears without self-awareness."

There are countless stories of animal apparitions from the feeling of the presence of a beloved pet that had passed away. To this day, I have yet captured one piece of evidence of any kind of animal spirit. It made me think about the bigger picture. If you are not vegan you probably ate, or wore something that had a face today, and most every day of your life. So when it comes down to animal apparitions, why is it usually limited to only our beloved domesticated pets? If I told you, human beings consume every species of animal greater than the number of human beings on this planet every year. When I listen to my audio for responses, the only sounds I have heard can only be described as human. Where are those billions of animals that we as a species consume every year, and yes, people have pigs, and chickens as pets? The most common domesticated pet kept by us is cats, but dogs are the most commonly claimed pet apparition. Are they smarter? No. Dolphins, Pigs, and Primates are smarter. Cats and dogs are way down on the list.

The only answer is us, and our minds ability to hallucinate as defined as perception at the threshold of consciousness in an awaken state, but this could explain away all ghosts? If it was not for one little problem, cameras, and voice recorders do not hallucinate. Although people can, and do in some cases that is why all evidence is subjected to peer review methods of evaluation involving qualified individuals within the relevant field that would provide credibility to the evidence, and if it wasn't for the overwhelming amount of the data that's been collected over the years we could end this discussion right now. I have personally witnessed on more than one occasion movement recorded on camera. Acoustical evidence as clear as someone speaking in the room called a disembodied voice, recorded movement as a locked door open, and closed, had one playing card move out of a deck of cards, a ball rolling back, and forth three times all caught on video. There are numerous claims of pet apparitions. The most recent captured on video that turned out to be a bug on the lens. A small blurry spot moved across the lens. That gave the illusion of something small moving across the room. There was the immediate assumption that the unexplained anomaly was an apparition of what was once a beloved pet that lived in the home.

People feel alone in their grief after the loss of a loved one. That trauma can manifests strong memories; you glance over to where your pet should be, to glimpse a memory of them sitting there, to look again to see nothing. This is what it means to be human and as researchers we must take in to account everything we know about how the mind works, and knowing that our mind can substitute memories at the expense of our reality. This is the main reason why we would never use sensitive, or psychics, and why we insist on backing up everything on digital recorders because by verifying the activity would mean the difference between a personal experience, and evidence.

I have seen confusion referring to the word manifestation, as if it only refers to a spiritual creation, and yet our mind is the seat of reality, and all of our manifestations.

Animal in the Paranormal (Sensitivity to the Paranormal)

Dogs are trained to use the animals since of smell to detect contraband such as drugs, or bombs. To attack and defend in law enforcement, or the military, but hunt for Ghosts? There have been claims that animals can sense activity associated with Ghost. The research I have done on our common household pets and their sensitivity to their surroundings. Let us start with vision, dogs are dichromats, and have color vision equivalent to red-green color blindness. Dogs have very large pupils, a high density of rods in the fovea, an increased flicker rate, and a tapetum lucidum an adaptation toward superior night vision. Dogs can detect a change in movement that exists in a single diopter of space within their eye. (Humans require a change of between 10-20 diopters.)

Comparatively dogs can detect movement that is up to 20 times subtler than human vision. The frequency range of dog hearing is approximately 40 Hz to 60,000 Hz, which means that dogs can detect sounds far beyond the upper limit of the human auditory spectrum. Additionally, dogs have ear mobility giving them the ability to pinpoint the exact location of a sound. Eighteen or more muscles can tilt, rotate, raise, or lower a dog's ear. A dog can identify a sound's location much faster than a human can, as well as hear sounds at four times the distance. Therefore, in conclusion man's best friend your household pet would be more likely to sense the presence of a small animal in the walls, or react to noises from outside passing cars or from other dogs. Some dogs barks almost nonstop when there is no apparent reason. Who is to say what they are reacting to when there are numerous more likely explanations than a Ghost? I have heard of paranormal groups training their dog to sense EMF. We already know that the world inundated with electromagnetic fields. All I can see are dogs running around with their owners while playing get the Ghost as easily as get the Frisbee or the ball. Theoretically, if there were Ghost the dog has far greater sense of sight, smell, and hearing to detect subtle changes in the room without the human owner sensing anything, but therein lies the problem. We would have no idea what the dog was reacting too. How can you train a dog to react to what we, as humans have yet to prove even exists?

Many of these trends are spurred on by paranormal non-reality TV shows in the attempt to keep the show fresh, and improve sagging ratings. As would the introduction of a dog for the president of the United States when approval ratings start to decline.

Chapter 11

The Cost of Ghost Hunting

If you are thinking about starting your own paranormal group here is something you should know. You should have a 'really good' day job because running a paranormal group is not cheap; equipment is in the thousands of dollars. Some of the more overly priced haunts cost over a thousand dollars to gain access to a potentially haunted site and this does not include food, transportation or lodging. The number of paranormal groups keeps growing every year. Some groups cater to people that only want to go ghost hunting. They charge ridiculous prices to join thirty or more people stomping around some alleged haunted location, and if you expect to get any real evidence from that, you are mistaken. Sometimes small groups like to meet in the cemeteries to walk around. I guess it is more for the creep factor than anything is, but when the sun goes down you need to leave. Cemeteries are under control of the Parks, and Recreation Department's Rules and Regulations. What that means you are not allowed in them after sun set. It's funny to see these amateur groups taking pictures of themselves obviously in a graveyard at night, and then posting it on *'facebook'* without bothering to get written permission, or permits to be there. I am sure the Sheriff's Department will be contacting them soon about the trespassing charges. Being legal should be the first of many rules for your team. Trespassing is dangerous should never be allowed especially when you can get permits and permission it may take some effort, but your team would have earned respect in the community. If you and your team ever has the need for that haunted fix. There are plenty of 'paid-to-investigate' haunts. That would more than happily gouge you for hundreds of dollars to walk around their alleged haunted property for a couple hours.

Then there are the Para-Conventions with their higher and higher ticket prices for the same old rehashed lectures that I have seen year after year. I spent the last one sleeping in the back row. The only reason we go to these things is to see friends from out of town. I would love just once attend a lecture with someone that can bring important innovation or insight to the field, yeah right! Then again, you might even see a Para-celebrity, and with fifty paranormal reality shows on air and new ones every year, you can take that bet to Vegas!

Then again, one of the funny things about paranormal conventions is when they throw in an investigation for an additional price of the ticket. What we call a stampede investigation, and are a total waste of money, and time. Forget trying to collect evidence when you have a hundred people stomping around, talking, yelling, knocking, pounding, and slamming door. Really, the joke's on you for paying money just to walk around the building. Most haunted venues charge teams $500 for the night. You and a couple buddies for a little more could of had the whole building to yourself for what they just charged you and a couple hundred people for that haunted experience. You've could of gotten the same evidence from a shopping mall for free.

My team spent the night at this overpriced out of the way Hotel that advertised their rooms as being haunted? In each of the rooms, there was a list of alleged personal experiences. Talk about selling haunted. The evidence that the Hotel was haunted was based on a group of psychics that claimed they saw spirits in every doorway. The Hotel built in the late 1850s, and what many people believe if it is old and creepy looking then it must be haunted? That is not necessarily the case after reviewing all the audio, and video from all our equipment we picked up nothing at all. Odd for a place that advertised as being so haunted to get absolutely nothing. Later we talked to the Hotel owner that admitted all the pictures and  stories were made up to add a bit of mystery and fantasy to the Hotel. I wish someone had told me that before I spent $140 of the worse night I ever stayed in a Hotel in my life, and you can keep the historical experience too! I am going to touch upon paranormal gear you cannot believe how much of it is worthless, and the worst thing of all! The manufacture even tells you so with four little words, for entertainment purposes only! I have seen groups walking around using those very pieces of equipment. What was worse is claiming they captured evidence from them?

Then you have the radio hacks these are so obvious on how they work. It is nothing more than a word generator by scanning through all the AM frequencies what you hear is words from News broadcasts, Talk Radio, and Religious Sermons. While the device is skipping through broadcasts, some frequencies are stronger than others are. Now ask a question all you need to do is 'pick up on' the loudest word that would best answer the question, and with all those names, places, and damnation it is not hard to convince yourselves your talking to the spirit world. If you're serious about the evidence all you really need for equipment is; video cameras as many as you can afford, stereo voice recorders with external microphone the reason will be explained in another chapter, trigger objects, and no more than six trustworthy, honest people. Only use photographs to document the location never as evidence. Uniforms are necessary in any profession along as there is a common theme, and don't wear rhinestones, or glitter on your clothing, they reflect as little points of light, and that's including infrared, and full spectrum, and yet I've seen teams with rhinestones on their shirts. "There was a lot of activity last night energy ORB everywhere!" The smallest reflective surface will reflect light back to the camera. I've seen an anomaly where it looked like ultraviolet light from a full spectrum camera reflected off something on someone's jacket when that person turned the flash blind the camera momentarily giving the illusion of someone vanishing. It is important to question all evidence if you want to be taken seriously.

Chapter 12

Paranormal Unity

The propaganda of Para-unity commonly used throughout the paranormal field. It has become the vehicle of choice by frauds, and bogus teams that only want to swindle, or promote their questionable evidence in the attempt to gain notoriety or fame. Originally, it was to share ideas, methods, and promote mutual respect throughout the paranormal community in the quest for the truth. The truth ended up with people using other team's ideas, and even their evidence to promote them self. Unfortunately, I have seen groups use the excuse of Para-unity to spy on other teams, or to spread disinformation about a specific group, or a specific person. Over the past seven years of running a very successful team, I have learned that the people around you are not necessarily your friends, and I have tried to keep out of all the Para-drama in this field as much as I can. The idea that any type of Para-union would work is flawed from the very beginning. There are vast differences between teams. Why would anyone think that groups with apposing ideas, methods, and training would ever work? Especially after seeing, what some of these groups consider evidence? Experience well trained teams tend to dominate over others. I agreed to assist a team on one of their investigation. I have been corresponding with the co-founder for a couple years little did I know that it was their second investigation. Talk about oil, and water. They panicked, and ask us to take over the investigation. We came to do the job, and provide our best to the client. Sadly, the other team only came to go 'Ghost Hunting.' We came up with incredible evidence within three weeks the promise we make to all our clients. The newbie team felt rushed after three weeks, so they only came up with echoes, even after we had heard, and dismissed the evidence as an echo. I managed to talk the client into another investigation. The newbie team felt embarrass so they insisted that we did not return for the second investigation. Collaboration between two or more teams can work successfully, but there has to be a lot of common ground for it to work seamlessly. If you look at all the opposing belief systems, just a simplest change in ideology has turned brother against brother. Personal ideology or beliefs systems are self-serving, and counterproductive. Methods of research preservation of the evidence, work ethics, and my co-founder Steve Watson pointed out that I run the team like a business. He is right! In a business model, everyone is on common ground. It keeps everyone focused on the project, and the problem at hand. It may help to get along with everyone, but it is not necessary, as long as you can work together. There is no drama in the workplace because there is zero tolerance, and the troublemakers immediately removed! One person's issues cannot be allowed to disrupt the team, and like all malcontent they immediately run to another team to spread their lies. Para-drama, it is to laugh! It is only from the very few, and the ones that deny it the most that are the biggest contributors.

There are many paranormal groups on social media pushing explainable phenomena. The most common mistakes are of camera anomalies. The blame lies with people not taking the time to learn, and understand their equipment from camera settings to the effects from the cameras flash, and other light sources. Does the manufactures recommend using the camera in low light? If you're standing in a totally darken room there is still indirect light you may not be aware of because it takes 30 minutes for the human eye to adapt to its low light surroundings called Scotopic Vision. It takes very little indirect light to briefly illuminate that "energy orb" dust particle, or bug that appeared then vanished! Then post those horribly blurred and smeared pictures claiming it is paranormal. If you had taken the time to learn how to use your camera you would have known that the shutter speed was set for low light that would explain those translucent spirits, and when using a flash that mist was in reality someone's breath.

You see nothing in the viewer

Until your finger is illuminated by the flash creating the shadow you did not see.

The shadow that was not there when you took the picture is your finger to close to the flash as in the example above. This field has some of the most novus attempts at photography I have ever seen. I have heard that there are no experts in the paranormal field. Okay so should we ignore all the other experts that can be used and rely upon in their respective fields for an opinion? Social Media is the forum of choice for the sharing of ideas, but when someone's ideas are so wrong that it hinges on delusional. When asked for comments and all you tried to do was to educate by providing a possible explanation. Taking great care to point out that they made an explainable mistake in the most nonjudgmental, and respectful way. Regardless of how delicately it was handled the first response is usually defensive; you was not there, how can you know? It is very rare to find someone that can except criticism, or agree with the explanation. Then when you intend to provide further explanation, it usually results in your comments being deleted, and even blocked from their 'facebook' page! Most paranormal enthusiasts prefer to believe that everything is haunted, and proof is everywhere. That is just not the case! Besides all the new or uneducated groups that rush to judgment with everything, they have caught turning the paranormal field into a joke. You have those other groups that purposely fake evidence for fame, and notoriety hoping to end up another Para-celebrity, or get on one of those Para-TV shows. Then if you weed out all the fakes, frauds, hoaxes, and the uninformed you just might find real evidence although it is very rare. None of which is definitive proof that ghosts exist!

Some paranormal teams come away with mountains of evidence every time they have investigated. The only way to explain this is if they based their evidence on unproven methods, and unrealistic equipment. Teams with psychics, mediums, and sensitive's tend to ignore explainable phenomena justifying camera anomalies, and the use of dowsing rods as credible evidence. It is easy for some teams to produce evidence that base their results entirely on fantasy. When a team investigates your claim, they should take every precaution to preserve the integrity of the evidence collected. That includes not having eight or more investigators in close proximity to each other preventing cross contamination. These teams encourage fantasy over critical thinking. Groups that cater to people that only wants to go ghost hunting. They charge monthly membership fees, investigation fees, equipment rental fees, and you get just that. Ghost hunting with no commitments. Just you and the other twenty-five plus members in the room with you "ghost hunting!" Groups like this are good at creating drama, and exaggerating airborne dust as spirit activity. Real paranormal groups expect commitment, and the only cost to you is your participation. That is if you are lucky enough to be able to join a professional group. Most professional groups have strict limits on the number of members they have. There focused on the experience, critical data, and the research gained. In professional groups, they expect the best from you. In return you learn new techniques, distinguish real evidence from fantasy. There are real answers to real phenomena, we ask how and why during our investigations because everything else is just sitting in the dark.

Many of the new paranormal teams I have seen contact the local News agencies to rush their unbelievable evidence to the public. They stand there with the reporter pointing at picture of Orbs, or slow shutter speed images claiming they captured a ghost. If you ever seen something that is reported on the News and they flash back to the studio knowing that these people are educated professionals with 20 years in journalism. I look for one of two reactions, laughter which means you just made a fool out of yourself, or serious reflection, which means you, said something that made them think, to a journalist that is everything. At any time you deal with the media, they will purposely try to steer you one way or the other. This is how you know if the reporter is looking for that quick laugh, or is serious about what you are saying. Unfortunately, not all, but most interviews I have seen regarding the paranormal, usually ends with a big laugh.

There are now self-proclaimed demonologists, and certified paranormal experts that are flooding the paranormal field. A certificate of completion means you completed a class there is no accredited institution in demonology, or paranormal investigations that can certify you in this hobby. The paranormal field has turned in to a cesspool of bullshit. It is difficult to make serious steps forward when you have teams that run around breaking the law, by breaking and entering, trespassing, stealing from locations they investigated, and then scaring people out of their homes because they have Orbs everywhere. I saw a video posted on YouTube where the team walked around with a cell phone ghost app that said the home had purple energy. When the client asked what purple energy is they did not know, but scary nonetheless. The biggest skeptic is you, and in research, you need to be that skeptic, except criticism because as hard as it is, criticism will make you stronger as a team, and will keep you honest.

The attitudes and immaturity in this so-called field are ridiculous. Teams threatening other teams for investigating in there town without their approval, or thinking that they can blacklist teams; it seems they think somehow they are so self-important that they have the power to do what? This is a hobby, god forbid the paid venues would not take my money? Most of these people are delusional I cannot believe what half of them say, as if they knew nothing at all about the world around them. The art of looking up information died with the art of debunking, or asking the simplest of questions. That when fairies and demons are accepted as logical explanations you might want to check in with your therapist. Fantasies are great in fiction when you turn off the TV, or leave the movie theater. That is when you need to get back to reality, and reality demands proof. Now we have teams faking pictures of ghost and are the easiest to identify because these are cell phone camera ghosts. Some of these are incredibly famous, such as "the lady of bachelor's grove" and is on almost everybody's cell phone. When called out for the obvious fake, the story changed from they caught it to someone sent it to them. I explained to a woman that claimed a ghost scratched her behind her ear. People unknowingly scratch themselves all the time. Why would you think that it is paranormal? She replied, "I know it's not a human scratch because I have been a nurse for the past seven years." How do you know that ghosts has fingernails when no one has proven that a ghost exists, and this is acceptable to you as an explanation other than someone had an itch and scratched it? The extent people go through to reinforce their beliefs is another social psychological trait by making their experiences more coherent, and orderly fantasy then becomes accepted over logic.

LAWS YOU SHOULD KNOW

It is illegal for anyone to be in a cemetery after dark. In addition, just because no one lives or works in a building, does not mean it is fair game for investigating. If you are caught trespassing, your respectability in the community is finished.

Cemetery LAWS

You should be aware of local ordinances to protect the public health, safety and general welfare. As well as regulations relating to the operation, control, and management of cemeteries.

The cemetery shall be open to the public during daylight hours as established and posted by The Township Board for the purposes of burials, graves visitation or historical research.

No person shall be permitted in the cemetery after dark except by written permission. This may include any permits from the county.

Any person, firm or corporation who violates any of the provisions of this Ordinance shall be guilty of a misdemeanor and shall be subject to a fine of up to $500.00 and/or imprisonment for up to 90 days in jail as may be determined by court of law. Each day that the violation continues to exist shall constitute a separate offense. Any criminal prosecutions hereunder shall not prevent civil proceedings for abatement and termination of the activity complained.

Trespassing LAWS

A person is guilty of criminal trespass if, under circumstances not amounting to burglary as defined:

The person enters or remains unlawfully on property; intends to cause annoyance or injury to any person or damage to any property, including the use of graffiti; intends to commit any crime, other than theft or a felony; or is reckless as to whether his presence will cause fear for the safety of another.

Is a class B misdemeanor unless it was committed in a dwelling, in which event it is a class A misdemeanor fine of up to $5,000, or imprisonment up to 7 years, or both for each violation.

Please check local ordinances for fines, and imprisonment for your county.

Remember local law enforcement and the **NSA** pays close attention to social media like facebook. Unless you do not mine being questioned, arrested or find for violating the law. Then I would not post such criminal activity.

The hobbyist should avoid clients and private property you can face legal, moral, and safety issues. You can also be held libel for all vandalism, theft, and damages. If all you want to do is go ghost hunting then paid venues abound and most of them have been featured on popular Para-non-reality TV shows. Leave those demons at home in your closet where they belong, or take the team out for movie night where monsters can frighten the bravest of you. It is better than being sued when you frighten the homeowner out of their house with talk of evil spirits, and cleansings.

The legalities does not end there is you are the founder of the team the felonies starts with you. You are responsible for anyone acting with or without your permission. The law will say that the member or members of your organization was acting on your behalf weather you knew it or not unless you have signed rules, and releases from each member that clearly states that you must have written permission obtained from the people named, and limit those names to the people you trust.

Paranormal Drama

The biggest reasons **NOT** to start a paranormal team are having to putting up with all the drama, and bullshit. It is easier, and cheaper just to hang out as a member of a team. There is little to no responsibility, unlike the founder of the team, members do not have to show up to every event. Another thing it is a lot of work, time, and money the members have little to no investment. I will endeavor over the next couple of paragraphs to reveal the truth behind running a paranormal team from a founders' prospective.

Where do we start?

Investment, the founder has everything to lose, and very little to gain. There is the time invested in each member after all the training that is provided for each piece of equipment, and software. Then I had a couple members that repeatedly come away from a five-hour investigation with no evidence at all? It becomes obvious that they want to play ghost hunter, but they are not willing to put in the work. As the founder of the team you made a promise to the client, and that is the reason why your there. You have a reputation that been built up over the years, and it all can be ruined by the actions of just one person.

Then there is the monetary investment in equipment; cameras, and audio equipment that I had to buy a cargo van to put it all in. Therefore, you would think I was serious about doing this. Something else you need to realize that you are the only one!

There are varying types of paranormal groups a few are research groups that are after data to explain phenomena, versus the other types that want to tell ghost stories, and spend their weekends walking through cemeteries. The point being that you have proven to yourself that what has been called a Ghost is real. That you do experiments, and create procedures to better collect evidence. Too finally have answers to questions that have been a part of human history for thousands of years, but doing experiments takes away from the fun. Now the truth comes out most of the people interested in joining paranormal groups would rather goof off, contaminating evidence voiding the reason why your there in the first place. There is that dollar amount it costs roughly $300 to $400 for gas, batteries, and that's not including equipment maintenance, ink, and other essentials every month to do residential investigations, not including the hundreds of hours involved in editing audio, and video to create a reveal set of DVDs for the client. The members only responsibility is to go through at edit their audio a lot of which is never turn over if anything is turned over at all. Well you are probably thinking that you are not looking for the right people. Well their all volunteers, and we cannot charge for our services, because there is not definitive proof that ghost exist. Therefore, there is no cash to pay anyone, and then there is the old adage; you get what you pay for.

The reason why you have members on the team is to share responsibilities. You know, people who have function, and purpose? Even though it turns out the purpose was to benefit them self. I brought in a person to promote the team, but after three months, they quit. All though during those three months had invited friends to our private investigations, and even instructed clients to use pagan rituals in their homes. After that member quit it turned out, they did absolutely nothing to promote the team during the time they were there. There had been a couple past members with little regard to the health, and welfare of the family by instructing them to use candles, and rock salt to rid themselves of the haunt.

You think that is fun 'I am just getting warmed up!'

How about deception, but on a scale that you would have to question their character, and believe me you don't what people with questionable character in people's homes, or representing you, or your team.

What do you think of someone that joins your team just to make the previous team they were with jealous? Showing that you cannot trust nobody I had the opportunity to be a part of a television show, but I needed a second storyteller. Therefore, I asked one of the members if they liked to do it. She said yes, then avoided discussing the show with me, and went as far as to claim she been diagnosed with throat cancer to avoid meetings. Only to later find out that, she introduced evidence that shown to be human speech, and when confronted about the evidence, resigned! She even went so far as to add another team she join a month after filming to the credits of the show.

Then there was the drama queen that played victim. The poor victim in this case asked to go to a church down the street from where she lived, and ask for permission to use an open-air chapel. Not only did she say she got the letter, but went as far as to post the content of this make believe letter online. Of course, we asked for the original letter. I scheduled meeting after meeting week after week excuses after excuses the team even met down the street from her home at the chapel, and waited for her to arrive, again without the letter. The victim said she forgot it at the house then she left never to return. I setup another meeting waited over forty minutes, and this is even after saying she would be there. I released her that afternoon that night the drama swung into high gear poor little victim she was so wronged. This was another member that said was hard at work on information for the team, but after repeated requests never delivered. We checked with the church they knew nothing about a letter, and are not even responsible for the open-air chapel. This is how one person can ruin a team's reputation.

There are some seriously deceptive people out there wearing as many faces as they did last names. She never stopped arguing, never stopped talking about people. The same people she now likes to call her friends. One evening my team and I went to meet with another team up north that shared a lot in common with us. Of course, it all recorded on video for prosperity. Unfortunately this person never stopped vilifying the team she was once with, and this other team that she felt had no place being associated with the organization they are with. The co-founder and I spent four hours trying to stop her mouth. There was that moment where I got her to stop only to have the co-founder asked her a question. **(AAUGH!)** Then we listened to her ranting until we all had to leave. I can only imagine what that team we met thought after all that. You never know how happy you can get after letting someone like that go. All the stress and drama she caused went with her! I can almost sleep at night.

I wanted to write this because there is usually only one side to the story ever told. I've been called the Devil because I respect truth more than anything else, and being an engineer it's a fundamental part of my profession to backup, and document everything, and when the truth is told fact speak louder than words, or in this case Screen Caps.

So if you like being made to feel like a doormat, or turned into the bad-guy. Even though you have made every effort to clear up any misunderstanding, so everyone can move on and yet that is another responsibility of the founder. Are you still interested in starting a paranormal team? It is better being a member of a progressive research team for the answers, unless you are in it for the ghost stories.

All this is what to expect; people as you have just read only want to use you, or use some part of you as long as it benefits them. I found a person I can trust to a large degree, so I made him my co-founder Steve Watson. There are good people out there if you can find them that are honest, serious, trust worthy, and if you ever come across someone like that, and they live in Northern California, send them my way.

Supporting Fantasies

Is your pet feeling troubled? Maybe your furry buddy isn't eating all the kibble. Well now, there is Pet Whisperers to ease your pet's mind! By simply removing that unwanted money from your wallet your pet will receive the full psychic experience. You'll see after the first visit a; shinier coat, less shedding, your pet will thank you as our amazing 12 step psychic treatment program works miracles on your pet!

FREE Pet Toy with Every paid Visit!

> **Pet's owner must be 18 or older, all miracles are suggestive, if miracle occurs there will be an additional charge, Cash only; For Entertainment purposes only!**

Harry Houdini in the mid 1920's was vilified by the Psychics, and Mediums he publicly expose to be frauds, and fakes. Houdini traveled from town to town-offering $10,000 to anyone who could exhibit supernatural phenomena. No one ever won the prize. Today James Randi self-proclaimed conjuror, Magician, and illusionist are offering $1,000,000 to anyone that can prove psychic phenomena, really! If I was so gifted I would at least be a Millionaire the money is still available. Over 90 years since Houdini called them fakes. Psychics and mediums are still hard at work. However, they justify charging for their act, by simply calling it for what it really is, entertainment.

Everyone as a certain level of intuition, some people are more intuitive than others are. All this really means is that some people have learned too quickly use their experiences to arrive at a course of action. Then there are people that claim to have the gift of clairvoyance, and would like to share their gift with the world, for a price? This part puzzles me. They can see the future, but they cannot come up between them with one winning lotto ticket? If I had this gift, I would be a billionaire! Then I really could share my gift with the world, without the need to charge people for readings.

I cannot believe how anyone can take mediums seriously, if the medium can talk to dead people and can pick up the presence of a loved one in the room then why asked anyone anything. Shouldn't the 'dead person' tell the medium who they are, and whose family they wish to contact? The medium should be receiving information not asking for it. Unless you have a weekly television show that is. Then let the bullshit fly! After all, it is entertainment, and people pay a lot of money to be entertained. As long as you realize that, it is a well-rehearsed act to fool you into believing them.

Psychics are just as bad I guess if you are into fantasy, and you have the money to throw away. When people are desperate, enough to go to a psychic it is because loved ones have been missing a long time, and it is their last hope. They need to know if a loved one is dead, or alive. When so-called psychics knowingly con people out of money, or give people false hope or no hope at all because all they are really looking for is that next paycheck that is when laws need to change or be enforced. There is too much fraud not enough people held accountable for it, and that includes paranormal groups some of them are worse than psychics at pushing fantasy.

I know of one family where the psychic told them they had a curse on them. They paid $1,200 to have the psychic remove the curse. Because curses, hexes, and demons do not exist, but fear can be a powerful tool when it involves you, or your loved ones. Paranormal groups are just as much to blame for encouraging a variety of beliefs, and mysticism.

We have heard from clients that had a paranormal team walk around the property then had a psychic contact them. When the psychic called, she claimed to 'Astral Project' herself over the phone into their home. Then told them they had angered the spirits, and charged them $300 for her services.

Why I am grouping sencitives' along with the rest of the frauds because perpetuating fantasies contribute to keeping the frauds in business.

"If you are not part of the solution then you are part of the problem." ~ Charles Rosner

I would seriously hope that before medical science publicly announces anything that would suggest a continuation of human existence without first putting in place legislation to protect society from the rush of con artist, and frauds already entrenched in this field.

Paranormal non-Reality TV

The catalyst that drives all the misinformation in the paranormal field lies squarely on the shoulders of all those paranormal non-reality TV shows. If I could get ghosts to respond on cue, we would then have proof that ghosts exist. Paranormal activity happens purely at random you will never know when or where it is going to occur, and even if you know exactly where to look the chance of catching the same activity at that location may never happen again. The only way to catch any of it is to have cameras, and voice recorders everywhere! Most of the time were sitting around talking to ourselves, and hoping for something to talk back. It is not all that entertaining in fact it is rather boring. I have been guilty of falling asleep on several investigations, and have slept like a baby-sitting in the middle of some of those popularized haunts seen on television. I was board to death!

Now try to make a weekly television show out of that, and keep your audience. You cannot without running around screaming, Aaah! Did you see that? Did you just scratch me! Now run around, and chase after something you cannot see? You have to wonder why shows like this are still produced. Regardless of which paranormal non-reality show you watch. Some to all of the evidence presented on the show been questionably introduced to some extent. People that have seen these paranormal non-reality TV shows do not realize that filming a forty-minute show where it looks like they investigated overnight, in reality took a film crew following your favorite investigator around on location an average of ten days. They stay in wardrobe wearing identical clothing during the filming, so in editing they match throughout the show.

Remember television is entertainment, but they go as far as appearing on other shows, or appear in public to claim that their evidence is real? Even after it has shown to have been faked, or staged! Then there is equipment used by these shows to communicate with the spirit world. In the real world, does nothing at all and you wonder why the paranormal field is in the shape that its in today.

It is funny when I am skipping through the channels and just happen across one of the more theatrical paranormal non-reality TV shows. I hear them replaying the audio evidence they caught. It sounds to me like garbled noise, and they immediately announce that it said something intelligent that came from a Ghost. I am assuming the distortion from their cheap audio recorder aids in the illusion of actually catching something. All these entertainment paranormal fringe-belief shows. They do not say they are doing anything real or telling any truth. The truth does not make money for them but supporting fantasies do.

Now with all these paranormal shows slowly dying off knowing that all good thing and many bad things that came from them will eventually come to an end. They all had a good run even though some of them will take a little longer to die. I can't imagine why some of these reality TV actors, and I use the word actor loosely, with all the years put in on these paranormal non-reality TV shows would respond with any skepticism about life after death. Seeing that they had limitless access to some of the most haunted locations in the world. That most of us could only dream about, unfortunately their full attention was on filming that non-reality TV show every couple of weeks, and themselves. Then after all those years, they came away with learning absolutely nothing even though some of them will continue to promote fantasies because of their reluctance to let go. These are the actors you will see ten years from now you know after all the fame and the money disappears, and they end up sitting in a mall somewhere in Los Angeles signing autographs like so many of the stars today that are forgotten tomorrow. I imagine it is difficult to collect falsifiable data with a camera crew following you around everywhere, but they had every opportunity to do something meaningful, but instead chose to promote fantasy in the pursuit of fame and fortune. Then again, any opinion from these actors should be ignored since the only evidence they ever collected was produced by the show for entertainment purposes, and that would pertain to each and every one of them.

Chapter 13

Object Imprinting

Earlier imprinting theories encompassed personal objects, belonging to a once- living human being, attaching their life force to the object. Some believe the spirit possessing the object, and of course, the story of the lost soul always turns out to be an evil dark spirit. The only recorded evidence of a doll moving was either faked, or hoaxed. You have to understand there is 90% fraud in this field but that leaves 8% questionable and 2% are currently unexplained. The number of the unexplainable events would be much higher if paranormal teams, and researchers took more care in collecting the evidence. Nevertheless, to say a doll cannot move on its own since I have never researched it. I do know object can store energy of a residual type, as in a Residual Haunt. In these cases, the human being imprinted their life force by repeating a routine for years on end. We once thought that Residual Haunts was caused when the imprinter died, and the activity continued. What we eventually learned is that trauma can be imprinted in different ways, and there is no need for a death. There is a Residual Haunt in which trauma is imprinted by the victims. In one particular case, the children were being physically abused. Therefore, fear played out repeatedly in the haunt. The owner of the residence knew the family, and they are all very much alive.

There is another case of a Residual Haunt where the property itself stored the event. It is not just in older homes, and you would have never known that the reoccurring activity ever existed if you never looked for it. We caught residual activity of a house fire that happened in 1974 completely by accident. We were interviewing a client around 11:30 in the morning and recorded kids screaming for help 'help me daddy' repeatedly for several minutes, we return at the same time weeks later and recorded the same event happening again. We learned that the house at that location burned to the ground. No one died there, but fear and trauma from the event repeated in an audio anomaly similar to electronic voice phenomenon every day. We can only assume that since the house was rebuilt that the energy from the trauma was imprinted in the minerals that are in the ground. Even though we have no explanation how these things occur in nature. Manmade electronic audio patterns are common ways to store all sorts of data from video, to audio the original media that was used for decades was common rust that was infused onto plastic tape. This is a common mineral found everywhere, but instead of making assumptions on the how it happen, or why it happened. Nevertheless, we will leave it to more technical minds to explain it. While doing an experiment at a home built in 1859 that was under restoration, I started looking at the materials in the structure to help me explain why this location had a very strong intelligent haunt. To try to explain how the anomaly was able to sustain itself for over 134 years. The wallpaper in different rooms during restoration exposed a unique wall construction made from redwood, and plaster. In the early 1800's the walls where covered in limestone plaster. Limestone has long since been theorized as a material that would sustain a haunt.

Lime plasters are typically composed of limestone, marble and quartz aggregate. Today Drywall is made from soft white or gray mineral consisting of hydrated calcium sulfate called Gypsum.

Help Me Help Me Daddy

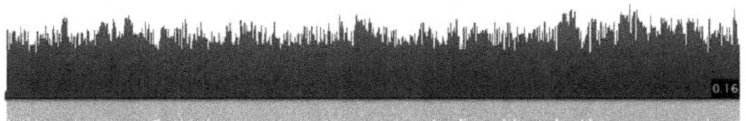

Soundcloud snd.sc/10su5Jo

In order to hear the low amplitude responses clearly you may need to turn up the volume, or put on headphones.

Porcelain Doll

The 19th century porcelain dolls not only are they the creepiest things ever, but the paint on them is high in led, and mercury. The horsehair originally used on the heads of the Dolls where later replaced with human hair because it was softer. In the late 1840s, the popularity of this Doll peaked with millions sold. This would have been a child's most cherished possession. The materials in the object, led for instance would lend itself to storing the bioelectrical pattern of the possessor. I have always have been fascinated by residual, or object possession. We have studied personal objects to see if the once living human being that owned it imprinted their bioelectrical pattern on the object. There are stories of haunted Dolls, where the head and arms move as though there still played with.

Again, I do not know what it is but Dolls have had a certain creep factor to them, but many of the older, puppets used in the early half of the last century had caricatures with grotesquely exaggerated facial characteristics. The most disturbing part was that they used these grotesque puppets to entertain children of the time. Dolls of the period did not fare much better with their misshapen heads, and the eyes that opened and closed. The creepy part is when the eyes open, when they should be closed. Nevertheless, for my sister sleeping with her dolls and stuffed animals were a nightly ritual that would lend itself to imprinting. We know residual haunts exist we have good evidence to support it. The question then can a doll be imprinted. Pointing out imprinting is not possession but a residual act that is repeated continuously in which the act itself repeats entirely on its own. If such things occur then there should be claims of haunted dolls? When referring to a haunted object most claims of a haunt are from the long fixed vacant look of the eyes in dolls, statues, and paintings that seem to follow you around the room, but are there claims that go way beyond the stare.

Out of the ten most haunted dolls, the top three are the most widely known and they are Annabelle, Robert, and Mandy. They are more an attraction at the museums that house them than anything else. I looked at other alleged haunted dolls some have video showing them move, one moved so much it should have its own paranormal non-reality TV show. The others are just old and that is about it just because its old does not mean it is haunted. Ebay sold one of the demon dolls, the one of the ten alleged most haunted dolls, and of course, an evil spirit possesses it. I am sure for the right price they will let you play with it, but remember to contact their psychic to have the curse removed afterword. The problems I have with objects that are haunted are the fantastic stories that surround them evil, curses, and demons remember to bring the kids they will have a blast. Why so cynical it is the mountains of bullshit there is so much of it that even if there was a haunted doll, and there might very well be. Only the naive would believe in it, causing the skeptics to make fun of it, and critical research to avoid it.

Annabelle Haunted Raggedy Ann Doll housed in a small cabinet in the Warrens Occult Museum. There is a sign on the front of the case 'warning positively do not open!' A crucifix and card that looks to have an image of the devil on it is attached to the front of the case. Strangely enough on the episode of Mysteries at the Museum, the curator opened the door held closed by a magnet. This unholy doll has the power to kill, claiming the doll was responsible for a death. The doll according to the stories can move on its own. Therefore, the dolls owners called in a medium who said the spirit of a dead girl Annabelle Higgins possessed the doll. Okay recap Annabelle this murderous doll kept in a case with no locks again held closed by a magnet. On a different video, the curator opens the case, touches the demon doll turns on a light inside the case. Again, dangerous demon possessed doll no locks and you have to open the case to turn on the light, you can touch it, and dust the Orbs off it without dying does not sound to me like much of a threat nonetheless another really good ghost story?

Robert the Doll displayed at the Fort East Martello Museum Key West Florida. The doll was given to the child Robert Eugene Otto when he was six by the Bahamian maid that allegedly practiced voodoo. The doll was named after the boy Robert. Growing up with the doll it was said that the boy talked to it, played with it, blaming it for all source of misdeeds keeping the doll until his death in 1974. When the artist was alive the doll was sat in front of an upstairs window that when children and neighbors walked by the home they reported seeing the doll moving about through the windows. There are other claims besides moving from giggling, and blinking to the expression on Robert the doll face seems to change. When the house was bought again, Robert was found in the attic. The doll became the owner of a ten-year old girl, who claimed to this day that Robert is alive. You would think with all the security cameras that should be placed throughout the museum and on Robert, the dolls case as well as all the paranormal investigations that there would be some corroborating evidence that would back up those claims. Robert the doll housed in a glass case as the doll sits visible from all sides there is a legend that if you take a picture of Robert the doll without asking first that the doll would place a curse on you. Sounds like a moneymaking idea to me. I can see a line of mediums patiently waiting for an unsuspecting family to take a picture only to be told that they now have a curse because they did not ask Robert the doll if they could take his picture.

Mandy the Haunted Doll lives at the Quesnel Museum. The previous owner claimed when she heard a crying baby she found the doll in the basement near an open window. After donated to the museum, employee lunches started disappearing from the refrigerator. Footsteps were heard when no one else was around, objects turned up missing, some only to be found later. Visitors to the museum report seeing her eyes blink or follow them around the room. Others claim to see her move entirely on her own. Okay let us blame the inanimate object for stealing lunches. Again, a good ghost story real or not will benefit any paid venue, and there are no shortages of ghost stories.

Chapter 14

Experiments Conducted (Cognitive Experiments)

We already have overwhelming evidence that suggests that the anomaly can see us, but we have not figured out how they do it, or at what level of clarity. We have gotten audio responses at other locations for the color Red, and Yellow.

Can the anomaly discern shapes are they able to see colors? Is the anomaly able to read, or is that a part of our physical self. At Meek's Mansion in Hayward California we set out to test the entities cognitive boundaries to see how much if any of our human consciousness remains after death. We know from previous investigations from EVP responses that an adult intelligent male anomaly believed to be William Meek. We know this from the many pieces of audio collected, and one in particular when the male voice asked for help from a family member, then his unknown niece Amelia. This response is one of many pieces of evidence that we know of that links an EVP to a once living human being.

What we found in our first cognitive experiments after reviewing all the evidence was that the anomaly could see colors, read, and answer questions from cards. Which in of itself is amazing? One other part of our cognitive experiment had the anomaly identify shapes. When we asked for a shape, the anomaly responded with "square" regardless of the shape that was on the card. I realized that the anomaly responded with the shape of the card, and not the shape on the card. Shapes were a disappointment even though we are sure that the anomaly can see shapes. It could be a problem seeing a two dimensional shape on a two dimensional surface of the card? We are not ruling out shapes until we try using three-dimensional shapes on our next cognitive experiment. Even though our results did not show definitively that, the entities can see shapes. We continue to explore other way's the anomaly can see. When we have better understood the entities, visual acuities. We will adapt our methods using what we have learned to communicate with the anomaly.

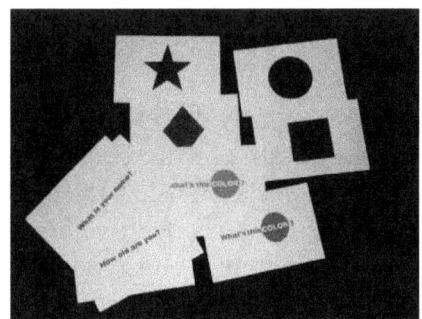

Cards used in Cognitive Experiment 1.

Cognitive Experiment 2

Returning to Meek's Mansion in Hayward California where we had so much success with our first two, investigations where we came away with incredible evidence. This time we brought eight three-dimensional wooden shapes in different colors. Three teams in rotation moving from floor, to floor. Each team provided with instructions on how to document the events throughout the night, and into the morning. Using nine tripod mounted Sony SR45 camcorders, two Zoom H2 four channel external microphones, one tripod mounted RT-EVP sound recorders, five Olympus 2x600/700/V40616 and one Sony voice recorders used that night.

<u>Shapes & Colors</u>

Circle	- Yellow
Square	- Blue
Triangle	- Purple
Octagon	- Red
Pentagon	- Green
Diamond	- Red
Oval	- Blue
Rectangle	- Yellow

Over a ten-hour investigation, taking us weeks to filter through 90 hours of video, and 90 hours of audio we found nothing that was unexplainable, or anything that we would consider a valid EVP. I know what you are thinking; you got nothing with all that equipment. Well nothing, we would consider being credible evidence. In any experiment, all evidence is thoroughly scrutinized because the results shape all future experiments, so everything is questioned. New methods created, changes made to the equipment, and the equipment deployment based off floor plans from the previous investigation. There is nothing more important than the credibility of the evidence.

We find it difficult to believe in a world plentiful in ghosts, and skeptical interpretations should prevail until displaced by strong evidence. It is very easy to be taken in by the hysteria of the moment. That is why logical thinking and reality checking should be a part of everyday research.

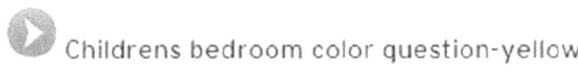

Childrens bedroom color question-yellow

Soundcloud snd.sc/12YJ7Hf

In order to hear the low amplitude responses clearly you may
need to turn up the volume, or put on headphones.

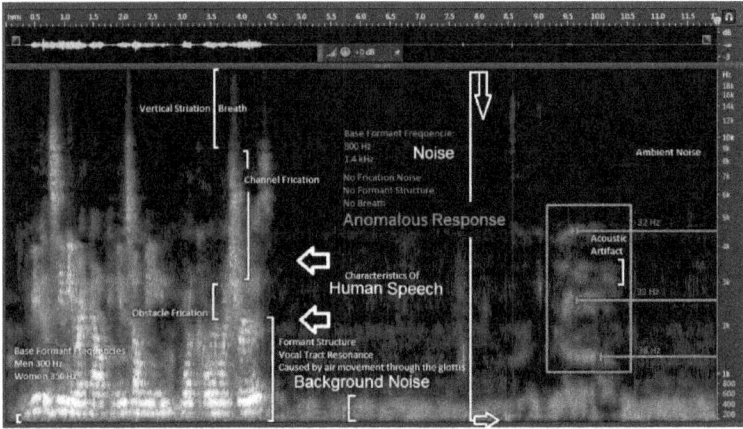

Again when comparing the formant between this EVP, and
Human speech in a wide band spectrogram. The formant in
the EVP shows no vertical striations by using the process of
Articulatory Phonetics for validating an EVP response.

Experiments Conducted

(Dimensional State Experiment)

Everything starts with a question. Marvin Scott 1999
WPIX News 11 interview Dr. Hans Holzer mentioned that
he believed in a continuing existence in another dimension.

How can you test for other dimensional beings? Well you
can only test within the limits of our own dimension looking
for characteristics outside of our own. How would the
dimensional being communicate with us? We do not know
if other dimensional beings exist. Since the nearest
dimension to, our own is the fourth dimension although
there is a hypothetical description of a fourth-dimensional
being from Princeton University.

"A four dimensional being can see across infinite three-
dimensional planes of space in a four dimensional world. A
four dimensional being would be spread across multiple
adjacent three-dimensional planes of space. A four
dimensional being could be taking up the exact space you
are, in. In the four-dimensional world, the four-dimensional
being could see you by looking across the multiple three-
dimensional planes of space to the one you are in. If you
could move past the four dimensional being in your three
dimensional space, it would constantly change shape. If the
four-dimensional being passes through your three
dimensional space you would only be able to see a three
dimensional cross-section that would constantly change
shape until it completely vanished. A four dimensional
being can see all sides of a three-dimensional object at once.
A three-dimensional object can generate two-dimensional
shadows on two-dimensional surfaces. A four dimensional
being can generate three-dimensional shadows on three-
dimensional perimeters."

"We live in a three-dimensional world. Although we can conceive of three-dimensions or less the one-dimensional line and the two-dimensional, surface it is difficult for us to imagine dimensions higher than three. However, mathematicians conducting research into space claim to be able to visualize four-dimensional space, and four-dimensional space can cast three-dimensional image, or a shadow of itself. At present, we perceive a rich world it has color, people live in it, and there is nature that extends out into space. However, if we consider this concept of light and shadow from a wider perspective, this world itself could be the shadow cast by some other great world. Early mathematicians perceived this as a possibility. The fourth dimension is the only other dimension that can cross through our three-dimensional plain of existence. Four-dimensional space can cast a three-dimensional image, or a shadow of itself."

By Dr. Michio Kaku, professor of theoretical physics at City College of New York

There is evidence in theoretical physics of a fourth dimension. A four-dimensional object should cast a three-dimensional shadow. In the paranormal field, we call three-dimensional shadows a full-bodied apparition. How can you test dimensional state of being, by looking for characteristics that do not match our three-dimensional existence? In the Princeton University description of a fourth-dimensional being, we looked for characteristics that we can test.

A four-dimensional being could see you by looking across multiple three-dimensional planes of space to the one you are in, and would be spread across multiple adjoining three-dimensional planes of space.

We planned this experiment at a known haunt. Where over the past couple years from 2010 through 2012 with four investigations at the location. We have had an ongoing dialog with an anomaly that was very consistent with its responses. The anomaly always responded when ask for its name, 'I'm David'
When ask what other names you went by it always responded, 'Dave'
Every question scrutinized for valid responses to eliminate contamination.

How to test Dimensional Theory

If the description of a four-dimensional being is correct, the anomaly can take up multiple three-dimensional planes of space. Then to test this theory we would need to ask simultaneous questions in multiple areas of the location. By reviewing, the audio for simultaneous responses would point to an existence outside the limits of our own dimensional state. While individual responses would point to a three-dimensional existence as in the one we are, in.

How the experiment conducted

Two researchers are setup at alternate ends of the location. Each researcher given identical set of cards with identical questions. We used knocks (*fig1*) to synchronize the asking of the questions because first we did not want to introduce any type of electronic interference that could contaminate the experiment. We found out on an earlier investigation that we could hear knocks from the other side of the location from the other team. Three knocks started the session, two knocks between fifteen-second pauses between the asking of the next question.

fig1

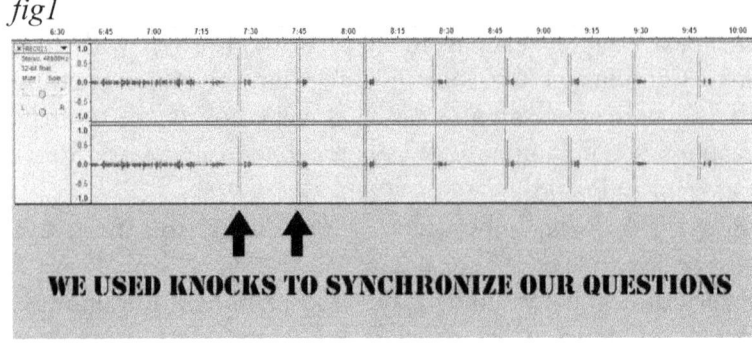

Results:

The DSB experiment conducted on October 6, 2011 from 10 PM to 11:30 PM after all power at the location was shut off to keep the noise contamination down. Comparing both audio recordings for responses shown in (fig2), we have concluded that the entity David is in a three-dimensional state of existence.

fig2

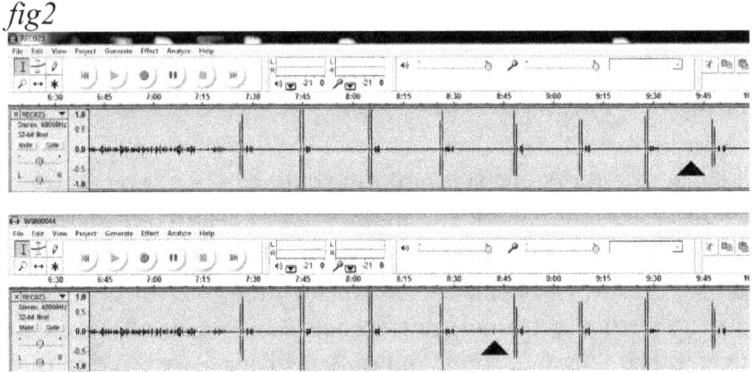

Even though the results from this experiment point toward a three-dimensional state of being, more experiments planned for different locations.

Experiments Conducted (Afterlife Experiment)

On his deathbed, Harry Houdini told his doctor that, even though he did not believe in spirit-communication, he would still try to send a secret prearranged message to his wife from beyond the grave. Every year for 10 years since his death, a séance was held every Halloween night, but on October 31, 1936, Bess Houdini announced, "My last hope is gone. I do not believe that Houdini can come back to me, or to anyone. The Houdini Shrine has burned for ten years. I now, reverently turn out the light. It is finished. Good night, Harry!" In 1941, there were attempts to record spirit voices, but it was not until 1956 that anyone was successful. In the early 1960s, the discovery of Electronic Voice Phenomena – EVP started the modern field of parapsychological research. Since then advances in audio technology has allowed communication from what we believe to be a once living human being.

Today we have an opportunity to conduct an afterlife experiment on a grand scale, due to the popularity of the paranormal field. In 2010, there were reportedly 1600 paranormal investigation groups throughout the world; a couple years later, that number has tripled. An entire generation that has accepted the concept of an afterlife, and that are willing to set aside the unpleasant subject of their death to participate in this experiment. As living beings, we must accept our own mortality, and that one day we will die. As paranormal researchers, we have experienced a consciousness that can exist beyond the death of its once living host, and believe that our conscious-selves can exist indefinitely.

This is not the first time anything like this has been attempted. There have been people that died clinically then revived to tell about it. We are not talking about a near death experience. There have always been some important underlying questions when capturing an EVP. Validating the response, which the book covers, is the biggest problem especially with all the amateur teams out there. Next, can we be sure that the entity is who it said it was? Big problem who the hell am I talking too! The last question is more about linking electronic voice phenomena to a once living human being. In chapter 9, 'Brief History of Electronic Voice Phenomena' that Dr. Raudive's deceased sister said her name three times, 'Tekle', and some voices addressed Raudive as his nickname, "Kosti" to validate the EVP responses. The problem I have is that maybe more than one person in the room knows these names. If I wanted to ensure that, the responses are, valid I would do what Harry Houdini did by using a code, or secret word that could be validated by third unrelated means. This experiment if conducted properly would prove that the entity is who it said it once was a living breathing human being with a name, a history, and a life.

Afterlife Experiment

Take a card print clearly one or more words, and that goes the same for numbers clearly on the card. What you have written must be unique only to you, and must never be forgotten over the course of a lifetime. However long that is. Now place the card in a self-addressed envelope taking steps to keep the contents of what is written on the card unseen even by looking through the envelope with a bright light, and then mail it to yourself. This is a method of using registered dating by the U.S. postal service for highly critical pieces of literature, thereby establishing that the material has been in one's possession since a particular date, and as long as the envelope remains, sealed can verify its legitimacy.

Written on the outside of the Letter. Upon my death, a professional paranormal team will perform an EVP session. This letter contains a single word that only I know. EVP question: What is written in the envelope? Only after three valid class A EVP responses clearly identified. Only then can a third party or representative selected by the family open the envelope.

Place the letter with your important documents for the long-term. Never tell anyone what was written on the card. Leave the same instructions in your last will & testament, so that your last wishes are carried out. One other way to add instructions without changing your will would be a handwritten letter with directions that are to be carried out upon your death. There are handwritten, or holographic, wills that must be written in only the decedents own handwriting. Check with your states laws on the legality of written wills.

Not relying on future trends or the longevity of organizations embedding enough flexibility in the experiment the final question is a simple one. The results of the experiment once completed, including methods of validating the audio are to be made public successful or not. Medical Science would have to explain, human consciousness, then the completion of research such as the AWARE study affirming that our consciousness can survive the death of its host. Showing data that links a once living human being to anomalous voice phenomena would be the final step in answering one of the oldest question that has been asked throughout human history is there life after death.

Chapter 15

Choosing a Paranormal Team

So how would you go about choosing a paranormal group to investigate your home or business? You should look for a local group with an online Internet presence with a minimum of two years, and ten, or more actual cases completed, and that includes turning over all evidence to the client. In this field, experience is everything. The group should base their investigations on hard evidence and scientific methods. Stay away from groups that use psychics, Ouija boards, dowsing rods, pendulums as their proof of activity. The group should have an impressive list of equipment and be well organized. A commitment to the client of confidentiality, and a three-week turnaround time on all evidence gathered. You should also find out about any liability coverage or waiver of liability in the event someone injured while doing an investigation on your property. Some of the other things you should look for are the professionalism, knowledge, and confidence of the investigator doing the pre-investigation interview. Remember to discuss your expectations, and any goals that you would like to achieve with the investigator. Also, check for flexibility when it comes to scheduling the investigation.

Reputable paranormal groups do not charge for their investigations. Payment therefore is the data collected. Well-organized group depends a lot on the number of years' experience in the field, the longevity of their members, and the skills each member can bring to the team. Evidence in the paranormal field is something that can provide an explanation supporting a claim or belief. We can capture unexplained activity, but the fundamental purpose for paranormal investigator is to give logical real world explanations for what been experienced. Not to prove a location is haunted!

Paranormal groups that are new in the field do not have the experience, or expertise needed to conduct, and complete their investigations. A lot of this has to do with people that treat is field like a hobby. People like ghost hunting but do not like to do the work. You need to keep that in mind when picking the right team for the job.

1. What you are looking for in a paranormal group?
2. Check for teams that are local to you.
3. Shop around there is different types of beliefs systems, or more evidenced based teams.
4. How long has the group been together?
5. Do they perform historical research?
6. Practical experience and research is important.
7. No one can guarantee to rid the location of the ghost.
8. The best way to deal with a haunt is to ignore it.

Any group that claims to have been around for years should have the experience, and evidence to prove it. Many teams equate years of experience with first encounters from childhood not actual research experience. We call this paranormal math because I saw a ghost when I was two years old does not mean I have 52 years of experience in the paranormal field. There is no such thing as a degree or certification for paranormal teams, or investigators. Established teams network with other local establish teams to ensure the quality of service for the area. References are always good some sites have pages of 'thank you' from clients that appreciating a job well done. Education in videography and photography is the type of training among members is something you should look for.

Teams in the paranormal field can be categorized as one or more disciplines listed below.

Fantasy Based: believe every location is haunted without first gathering proof. Relying on the intuition of psychics, sencitives, and mediums to dictate reality. Fabricating evidence where none is present. Relying on unproven methods, techniques, and equipment as proof. Refusing to accept explanations for common phenomenon preferring instead fanciful explanations.

Belief Based: practice religious or pagan rituals in the attempt to end the haunt. Poorly educated use of equipment, along with symbolic artifacts that do no more than reinforce their beliefs as evidence. Making conclusions solely on beliefs excluding any pretense of critical thinking.

Research-Scientific Based: the use of equipment without learning how the device actually works. Basing evidence on equipment, and software with the assumption that the data is valid when in all actuality does nothing at all. Making the claim of following scientific methods without understanding the process, or forming methods of research and procedures to insure the validity of the data. Absents of all critical thinking.

Skeptical Based: disproving all data by focusing on the obvious frauds. Forming explanations regardless of any falsifiable data that is available. Making cynical remarks arguing that it is all fantasy by ignoring documented research from university studies, physicist, and trained professionals in there selective fields.

Study Based: strict documented methods and procedures on conducting every aspect of the research from equipment deployment to validating, and falsifying all data collected. Conducting experiments that makes predictions along with single, and double blind studies. Having qualified experts in a peer review process for all data collected. Knowledge of all specifications, and operating parameters, on all equipment used.

In general, if a group considers themselves professionals, it should be their intention to present the truth to the public that visits there website or other public forums? If so, then they should be accepting and even eager to have a skeptical person along with them not the kind that say they are skeptical, then are the first to scream ghost. Otherwise, shunning skeptical minded people would say to me that their group is not confident in their work, and that they just may be deceiving the public that goes to them for help. Why? Those groups that deliberately exclude skeptics who debunk their evidence, it means their evidence is invalid because it has a natural explanation and that they are hiding that fact. When a paranormal group actively shuns skeptical thinking, they simply cannot be trusted and are not worth your time.

Chapter 16

Methods' and Procedures

In this chapter, I put together every method and procedures that has shown results. As well, as need to know information about managing a paranormal team, and insight on equipment I used.

Turn off Auto-Gain. While listening to the recording, you should note if the background noise appears to fade drastically when a real, loud sound happens. This means that your recorder probably has an auto-gain circuit (AGC) whose job is to keep sound levels roughly constant. Most voice recorders have AGC, and in most models can be switched off. Last thing you need is to have your voice recorder fading in and out when picking up sound especially when the sound is at a frequency below 50 Hz.

Turn off noise cancelling headphones. Noise input from the microphone inside each ear cup, sense and generate a "fingerprint" of the noise, noting the frequency and amplitude of the incoming wave. Then they create a new wave inside of the ear cup from the speakers along with the normal audio that is 180 degrees out of phase with the waves associated with the noise. Introducing noise meant to filter out low amplitude sound waves merely masks out the low volume sound that you are wanting to hear.

The Walk-through

One of the most important things we do before committing to an investigation is a walk-through. Floor plans drawn up during the walk-through will help in deploying equipment, and point out hot spots. During our walk-through, we take control shots, run video, and audio conducting an EVP session as a paranormal type of litmus test to determine the level of haunt, or if there is any haunt at all. We have picked up great evidence during our walk-throughs.

Historical Research

Historical Societies: (lineage, and Genealogy)
Libraries: (Old Documents, Newspapers, and other printed materials)
Museums: (Local History, Photographs, and Maps)
Real Estate Records: (History of ownership, and disclosures)
County Records: (Marriage License, Birth, and Death Certificates)

Research is vital to understanding the haunt! What usually starts as a Mystery? This is when having an Historian on the team pays off. Hundreds of hours spent in Libraries, and Museums chasing leads. What we end up with is the real Ghost Story.

Control Shots used in part with both videography and digital photography as a process to document locations. Proper documentation can establish the precise location and relationship of objects and evidence. A control shot is a duplicate shot of a scene from which video evidence is recording, or where photographic evidence is in question. It is the purpose of documentation to record and preserve the location and relationship of discovered evidence as it was when, the documenter was observing it.

Types of documentation you should have you can find online are:

Membership Documents
Confidentiality Agreement
Liability Waiver
Emergency Contact Information
Minimum Equipment Requirements
Membership Requirements
Release of Likeness
Waiver of Liability
The other documentation you will need is client release of liability:

Client Documents
Letter of Interest
Permission to Investigate
Initial Contact Report (Phone Interview 1)
Client (Onsite Interview 2) Questionnaire
Release of Likeness
*Confidentiality Agreement
Liability Waiver
Thank You Letter

Remember to give them copies. In the 'Confidentiality Agreement', there should be previsions for data collected. Making sure that the client's privacy is safeguarded, but all evidence should belong to you. If you capture incredible data, you should have full rights over it. This is the cost of being FREE of charge.

Keep noise contamination down!

We get just as much evidence during the Day, as we do with the lights on, or off. The big advantage to investigating at night is noise! Since most of the evidence you catch are EVP! Noise of any kind even outside noise, if prevented will save evidence. What do I mean save evidence: Training to keep your voice down and that is everyone? Not to walk on someone EVP, we wait 15 sec after asking the question in silence relaxing our breathing and even holding our breath for the 15 sec. Tag any unavoidable noise! We use a decibel meter where we train people to speak at a moderate tone around 50-60 dB, we have a saying "Their dead not deaf" No yelling out your questions, No whispering, No playing around when someone is asking questions. Most likely, the entity you are screaming at is standing right beside you.

The microphones on most audio recorders are mounted inside the case. Therefore, anything touching the case including your fingers when holding the audio recorder is picked up as noise. Using an external microphone on your voice recorder will eliminate those noises. There are brands that have external microphone built on top of the audio recorder such devices are the high-end studio recorders.

Geophones or (seismometer) can pick up the slightest movement, or vibrations by lighting up any number of Red LEDs on the circuit board mounted to the top of the project box. This device in the paranormal field comes in handy I have four of them. Place one of these beside your trigger objects to rule out vibrations, and movement. Remember weak floorboards, and subtle seismic activity. This device is so important in debunking evidence for that reason I am going to show you how to build one in the Easy Equipment Projects of this book.

Our **equipment standards** based on 'no power' locations, and that includes unattended investigations, 24-7 30 day capable so that we can accommodate anyone any time anywhere. It is important to be as flexible as possible, so that we can meet any of our clients' needs, and concerns.

Unattended Investigations

Programmable robots that can journey into unsafe areas or locations that the client cannot allow anyone in unattended or there is a question of liability in areas overnight. These robots can do EVP sessions; some are controlled from anywhere that has Wi-Fi, or robots that sense their way through the location.

Shutting of the power

There are advantages in shutting off the power if the client lets you do it. Electrical noise that hum, click, crackling noise that you hear in the background. Home appliances, electronics of all kinds if you can unplug, turn off, and disconnect everything! See if they let you shut off the power. We investigated a business that we had them pull the power more than once or there would have been no way we could have investigated. The hum from the electronics in the building produced noise 170 Hz wide at the 1 kHz range distorting any possible response. It is time to whip out the

Ouija board because you are not picking up anything with that going on.

The poor man's copyright - CYA

Is a method of using registered dating by the postal service, a notary public or other highly trusted source to date intellectual property, thereby helping to establish that the material has been in one's possession since a particular time? The concept is based on the notion that, in the event that such intellectual property were to be misused by a third party, the poor-man's copyright would at least establish a legally recognized date of possession before any proof which a third party may possess. This is very important I have had someone already claim the content of my first book. He first asked me to use it and I said okay as long as he gives me credit. Later I started seeing my content used in his videos, and internet radio show claiming himself as the originator. You cannot trust anyone always have a written agreement upfront before giving anyone permission to use any of your content.

Scheduling Procedure

Steps in scheduling an investigation,

1) Activity Report filed online from our website by the future client.
2) The case manager sets up a phone interview.
3) The case reviewed by the team.
      a) At that point, it either is accepted, or turned down!

Remember we reserve the right to refuse service to anyone. It is for our own safety

4) If the case is accepted, the walk-through scheduled with the client.
5) Walk-through a small team of two or three members arrive at the location.

- One member begins an interview starting an audio recording that later reviewed for possible EVP evidence.
- Second and/or Third member(s) walk around the property, a floor plan created marking hot spots, hazards, and hidden spaces, anything the team will need to know for the investigation. Pictures taken along with the floor plan to help with equipment deployment.

All findings reviewed, discussed along with any concerns from the investigating team before scheduling an overnight investigation with the client. One very important condition is necessary. Everyone except the homeowner must vacate the property to limit audio contamination. The sounds from the location are a fundamental part of the evidence, so we take every precaution in reducing noise contamination.

EVP Procedure

Remember the EVP rule is pause between each question for 15 seconds, and accompanying researchers must observe total silence. The only exception is tagging unavoidable noise. Take turns do not talk over each other's EVP and practice relaxed breathing if you are a heavy breather hold your breath during the 15 seconds pauses. Drink plenty of water to keep stomach noises from occurring.

1. Take your EM reading as soon as you enter the area looking for high EM fields that can cause illness.
2. Speak at a consistent and moderate tone of voice 50 to 60 dB (No whispering)
3. Avoid making any noises during the sessions (tag any noises that you are responsible for, or any other unavoidable noises, or contamination.)
4. Keep questions short and to the point.
5. Keep language within the period, and history of the location.
6. Avoid asking YES/NO questions.

The questions attempt to encourage the entity into giving you useable information.
Try asking them to tell you about their lives.
Ask questions that would interest you, or encourage you to answer.

Start each EVP session with {number} the time is {time} {location} {area}

NOTE: take temperatures during session.

Each accompanying researcher must state his or her {name}.
(Used as a voice record for debunking)

Introduce yourself

My name is {...} I am your friend. I am here to talk to you. Can you approach me; get as close as you can to me, and talk as loud as you can into this 'tool' it can hear your voice. (We found playing the friend card worked)

This tool cannot harm you in any way; it is the means to communicate with you. We always use the word tool because it is easily recognizable in any era, unlike device, or voice recorder.

Have as much history on the location and have already compiled a list of questions.

If you inadvertently ask YES/NO, question. Just follow it up with a WHEN HOW WHAT WHY and WHERE.

Evidence Review process begins at the end of each investigation. All members expected to assist in evidence review. If you have evidence from an investigation, you must present the evidence to the group within two weeks of obtaining it. If given evidence to take home to review you are responsible for that evidence. If you need help in completing the review of the evidence, you are to let us know right away so that someone may help you to complete the review. Being late or negligent in turning in evidence may result in forfeiting your opportunity to participate in the next scheduled investigation. We made a commitment to the client that we would reveal the evidence we collected within three weeks after they trusted us, and invited us into their home.

Floor Plans

Floor Plans are necessary for many reasons. First, it is important to mark down all the locations of where the claims of activity occurred. This can help identify patterns that could explain the activity such as exposure to high EMF or the lesser-known CO_2 poisoning. It is known that high EMF can make you sick, but Carbon Monoxide is odorless or colorless, and can cause the same symptoms the only differences is that CO_2 can cause death. If the activity focused in a particular area, a floor plan would point out a location of interests.

Secondly, equipment deployment that means strategically placing equipment from your arsenal to improve your odds of catching activity. This is critical since you never know when or where it is going to occur. It is always a good idea to have the odds in your favor. Finally yet most importantly showing equipment placement will aid in debunking activity if there's ever any question on what is caught during evidence review. This will also keep you from losing equipment when it is time to retrieve it.

Team Conduct

Any conclusion without supporting evidence is baseless, and never given to the client. We should always conduct ourselves as professionals exhibiting a courteous, conscientious, and generally businesslike manner at all times. Remember the client is always watching.

Never draw any conclusions to what you may have experienced during, or after the investigation to the client. (If the client asks what we have found tell them we will need to review all the audio and video over the next three weeks. Then we will review the evidence with them in person, and try to answer all their questions.) Anything you may have thought, felt, or saw is irrelevant without evidence to back it up, and comes down to a personal experience.

Watch what you say at all times! The client is always listening! What overheard, even in idle conversation can be misunderstood. During intentional conversation, you must be clear! Everything explained to them during the reveal process. The client will have an opportunity to ask any questions they might have about the data at that time.

Provoking is a technique to annoy the ghost into getting evidence. If all you want is evidence, it is a very valid way to achieving it. If it is not a private residence, let us say a location that most of the time is vacant no one lives there, like large paid venues, provoking works. The evidence collected using this method in every case showed a very powerful angry response, and is some of the best evidence I ever caught.

Trigger Objects

We have had allot of success with trigger objects attracting, and capturing paranormal activity in front of the camera. We have tried different methods to attract activity, but without the use of anything to focus the camera on! If the activity is from a once living human being (ghost?), then curiosity is without a doubt one of our strongest human traits. So what are people curious about, what would get you to stop, and look? We have used toys, balls; money from the period, the best evidence was from playing cards. By researching the background of the entity haunting, the location uncovered a sweet tooth, so we planted treats in location of the entities death. We find trigger objects to be very useful.

At the Gold Hill Hotel in Gold Hill Nevada there where claims of children playing in room 12. Trigger objects of a ball, and a deck of playing cards was set out to catch any activity. What we caught was one card moving out from the bottom of a deck of playing cards without moving any of the other cards in the deck. This is the video footage of the activity caught in Room 12 on our YouTube channel at spectroinstitute.org.

At Preston Castle on the second floor in what once was Anna Corbin's office we placed two dozen roses alongside a ball, and asked Anna to move the ball. After the team left the room the ball moved back and forth four times returning to its original starting place. There is video footage of the activity caught in Anna's Room on our YouTube channel. There was a question about if the floor was level stating that if the wind moving through the room rolled the ball up an incline then rolled back. Well we returned to Preston Castle to answer that question.

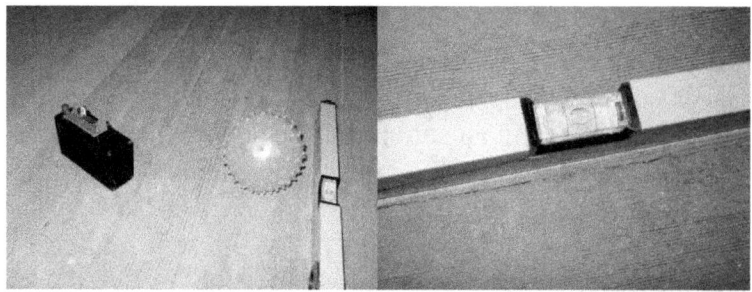

As you can see from the photograph above the floor is perfectly level, and the wind that was claimed to be moving the camera was nothing more than the auto focus moving in and out giving the illusion of movement. Therefore, in conclusion, since it was a Ping-Pong ball and weighed nothing if the wind moved the ball then why did not it simply rolled away instead of rolling back four times.

Support equipment, such as a level, simple air streamers, or a *geophone* placed alongside of the trigger object such as a ball for example, can help debunk claims of external forces causing the event. Placing these simple tools in the room will help support your claims of catching paranormal evidence, and can help in debunking the event.

Mel-8704

Paranormal Device that measure EMF and temperature. Gary Galka (designer) named the device after his daughter Melissa who died in an automobile accident in 2004, so the device is named Mel-8704 after the birth and death of his daughter.

Recalibration

Step one: Hold REC/ENTER and HOLD/ESCAPE buttons down at the same time. Turn the meter on while you continue to hold the above buttons down. When the meter turns on S-ON will appear.

Step two: Release the buttons and zero will appear, quickly press the up button until 9 appears and press enter.

The number 100 will show up and the numbers above it will move allow 5 seconds for the numbers to stabilize and press enter. 200 will show up allow 5 seconds for the numbers to stabilize and press enter. 300 will show up allow 5 seconds for the numbers to stabilize and press enter. Turn the meter off. Now turn the meter on. 0.0 should displayed if the calibration was good.

Chapter 17

Types Haunts Encountered

The common types of haunts are personal haunts. That most personal haunts stem from very rational explanations such as mental illness, medications, or fantasy prone personalities. We hear many claims that are for the most part creations of paranormal non-reality TV shows.

Actual haunts fall into a couple categories from residual haunts that a repeating events without the capability to interact with anyone. Then there are the ones that are not all there cognitively. They are confused, and frightened are usually the recently deceased, we have recorded an angry response from an entity after one of the researchers rummaged through what could of possibly of been the previous owners personal property. This was from an obviously very intelligent entity that showed emotions, and cognition. Intelligent haunts are rare the ones we have tested show amazing cognitive abilities. Some of the most bewildering is the ones that can learn even though only momentarily. As you well know there is no physical presents at least nothing that can be seen. One of our blind physicist friends that had listened to our audio joined us on a couple of investigations, and even after telling us that it was, the best evidence he ever heard had no explanation.

Mischievous ghosts are common in most homes with young adults and children the entity wants to play games. Although the activity is at first playful usually ends up frightening the family. The claims that reported are categorize as tormenting from touching, moving objects, and mocking all very childish behavior. At the location, we caught a clear EVP of mocking directed at one of the researchers. He heard a noise down the hall then responded with; "What the hell was that?" The entity then repeated the same, mocking the researcher.

Ghost Mocking

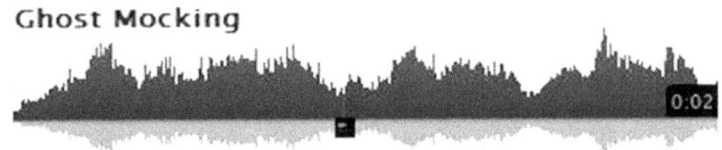

Soundcloud snd.sc/P5dfWO

These types of haunts usually described as demonic. The Devil and Hell are Christian concepts we have never found anything demonic, unlike what people will tell you. All entities should be categorized by their haunt. Intelligent haunts are described by showing feeling and emotions as if they were a once living human being. I have never, nor has any of my team or colleagues ever experienced anything demonic. Of course, there are all kinds of unsubstantiated stories. Back before there was the internet, there were these buildings of great knowledge called libraries, and unlike rumors, to the contrary they are still here today. I would like to encourage you to visit one and educate yourself on the origins of such things.

Next, there are the ones that are in denial they will tell you they are not dead. Then we have the others that will tell you not only are they dead, but how they died. Every entity we encounter vary in strength, and ability some are very aware with astounding cognition. Most of the time responding in bursts as if they need time to regain their strength, and then do so selectively. Others are limited due to the era in which they lived it is common to be asked, "What are you doing?" with the occasional expletive thrown in for good measure.

Chapter 18

What do we really know

There is the popular concept that the entity is a pocket of energy, but when everyone believes in a common explanation, leaves no room for alternative ones, and without new ideas, we will never know. On very rare occasions, we have captured anomalies that just do not mesh well with mainstream society. There is no proof that a 'Ghost' is the cause, or even if they exist, but there are clues, what do we know for sure. To say we know nothing at all gives us a foundation to build on. There are no rules, no handbook, religious dogma was more meant to rule the fearful, not the learned. We have asked every possible question, and questioned everything. Let me make it clear that once we die our physical self-ends. Everything in time becomes a distant part of the past until even the contributions you have made in life turn to dust. Immortality therefore is merely an illusion, an afterlife with angels are merely stories. There is the unexplained because no one has earned the knowledge, but instead clings to baseless fantasies. Even when logical real world explanations are clearly apparent there merely tossed aside when it interferes with beliefs, or fanciful explanations. It seems that most folks out there just seem to prefer to have fantasy and deception rule them. Because of this real science has given the question of a possible continued existence a great deal of distance labeling research in this field a pseudoscience with good reason. Any serious research lacked critical thinking, evidence lacked credible data, and observations lacked documented proof.

Skeptical, then again why blame me, the majority of the claims of evidence are either faked, fraudulent, or fantasy.

Therefore, when real evidence comes along, it is just swept away with all the rest of the bullshit, understandable! There are answers for most alleged spirit activity. On rare occasion, you come across the unexplained, real evidence that demands a second look. Medical science is on the verge of exploring beyond the limits of what our current knowledge has yet to explain.

What I have learned by researching hundreds of locations are what I and my team have experienced is very real. It's because of the skeptic in me, that forces me to take that step back, and think about what is going on, what was caught, and if it's explainable. After all, if there were not some truth to this I would not be doing it. I am not one to believe in ideals from a long dead culture thousands of years before science. I know that our mind plays tricks on us every day, and what is worse is that we ignore a large part of it. Most people are content to carry on with fantasy, because reality is too much trouble. What are we after credible evidence of course? How are we going to find it? Hours, and hours of recording meaningful data from equipment that has yet to be built, and money that would be better off spent on life, and the living. If it was not for that one annoying little thing, that everyone on this planet will one day face, and that is death. So now, you are thinking well there nothing you can do about it. You die, you are placed in the ground, and that is that. Unfortunately, nothing is ever so simple, especially when you dig through thousands of years of religion, myths, and recorded human history. Some believe that you see a brilliant light; the ones that do not cross over are stuck here? I am still trying to figure out the crossing over to where part.

There is the highly controversial method of communicating with the dead called Electronic Voice Phenomena - EVP. Which in and of itself, is self-defeating if you do not know how, or what to look for when validating the response.

Although the valid responses you get can tell a completely different story. We have encountered very intelligent responses from entities using this method that show cognitive ability, observational skills, and can respond in complete sentences. Most of them knowing that they are dead some date back over 150 years, in California that is a long time. This to me proves that a small part of us lives on after death; would you call it an afterlife? It is not an ideal one! There are limits not just the obvious physical one, but the end of the physical mind has the biggest impact. They are only aware of their own little era of time. When asked what year it is, it is always the last year that they lived not the current year. They remember being sick, or having a heart attack, and yet some do not even know that they are dead. One particular entity his name is David told us the last thing he remembered was a kiss. So much for "Ecclesiastes 9:5 but the dead know nothing" it is surprising how much is still there. My team and I have experienced a full range of emotions from the happy helpful entity all the way to the point when we pissed it off. Nothing to violent, however they are able to move objects up to ten pounds although others have witnessed an 80-pound wrench picked up out of its steal brace and thrown to the floor. Occasionally an object been witnessed thrown across a room. I and other Researchers caught on video being push, touched, and hit. The entities are more vocal than physical I imagine it takes more energy than a couple death threats, and believe me I gotten everything from "I'm going to kill you", to "I want you dead."

Experiments on cognition the results showed an ability to read, follow written instructions, and see colors. We have good evidence that they can see even though the last cognitive shapes experiment yielded nothing.

Dimensional state of being experiment showed that the entity is three-dimensional like us, having to move from point to point, and place to place.

The speed of the entity is indefinable we recorded a deck of playing cards at rest and within 1/35 of a second a single playing card from the bottom of the deck moved out without moving any of the other cards. This was not an isolated incident, but the second time I have seen on video an object moved that fast from one state to another. The difference in time between those two occurrences was at least seven years, and 80 miles apart using different cameras.

Our ongoing research has yet to determine if the entity can learn beyond its point of creation. The nearest thing that was observed was repeating our name or piece of equipment even though it was only momentarily, nothing long-term. There is the obvious limitation that without a physical source the entity has no way to store long-term memory. Until at some point, we have some conclusive evidence to the contrary.

The astounding thing is the entity seems to be very intelligent, has shown a limited form of comprehension, full range of emotions, verbal communication skills including foreign languages if known in life, shown visual ability, and is able to move objects without the need of a physical self, and yet when going outside of the entities era of comprehension. Confronted with new words, or objects is usually met with confusion, and frustration. The entity recorded lashing out! Physically by pushing, hitting, and throwing objects, as well as verbally with the use of profanity, and the occasional death threat directed toward the researcher. Overall, it is a very human response under any condition breathing, or not. The entity projects itself with very human characteristics it would be difficult to say if the entity is imitating human beings, or was once human itself.

Theory of why an apparition is depicted wearing clothing. – By Edward Krietemeyer

There is the question of why an apparition is described wearing clothing? The apparition is nothing more than mind a conscious form of energy, our physical self-decays. The once living human being reduced to its last cognitive state. The entity projects an image of how it last perceived itself at the point of death. Throughout our day, all short-term memory processed as long-term physical memory. As we sleep our brain cycles through memories, reorganizing connections while strengthening proven connections between brain cells, and our synapses. We wake up feeling refreshed, and restored ready to begin the day. Our conscious self-starts over. We make new choices, what to wear, what to do, with whom we will interact, and then consciously, and subconsciously organize our daily routine. Each day we start with a fresh perception of ourselves: how we look, what we wear, where we go. If you were nothing more than the sum of your experiences of the last day you lived, then you would project an image of how you last perceived yourself. This is why apparitions depicted as having a human shape. We view ourselves as having a head, arms, and legs, and even visualize the clothes we last wore. As our presence disrupts the atmosphere surrounding our conscious self, we project the image as we last viewed ourselves.

Our eyes see a very small range of the electromagnetic spectrum called visible light. Wavelengths above and below are unseen. There are limitations in the eye's dark adaptive abilities which includes sensing movement our vision is very poor when it comes to motion, and the dark. Depending on how it moved and at what wavelength there could be a whole other hidden world that could exist around us, and we would not know it.

Targeting Audio Devices best supports observations.

The difference between an electronic voice phenomena and a disembodied voice is the amplitude in the sound wave. The greater the amplitude the more energy used, and the louder the voice which would explain why most voices recorded are low amplitude. (-40dB to 60dB)

I have always thought that the entity was stronger at night, but that is not the case. People report activity happening at night because of parasomnia, and the stillness of the night. Noises that you would normally ignore during your busy day in the quiet of the night become eerily creepier. That is the primary reason why paranormal investigators turn off the lights is for the creep factor. Realistically the same activity caught at night occurs during the day.

On two completely different occasions, heat was a factor. The clients seen full-bodied apparitions both of the rooms had temperatures above 90-degrees from poor ventilation. I witnessed at one of the locations the doorknob turning the door opening then slamming back in to the doorframe bouncing open as the doorknob released. I went back a couple days later after I reviewed the audio, and video to try to debunk it. The only way the door would not luck after repeatedly slamming the door was to duct tape the doorknob turned to retract the bolt, and then pushing the door into the doorframe until it bounced open with a gap of two inches as it appeared on video. Look up Newton's second law of motion. At the other location, doing an EVP session I was talking about if heat played a role in projecting an image of themselves since in both locations the clients saw full-bodied apparitions. When listening to the audio I got a reply 'absolutely!' The co-founder and I have found it useful to ask questions about equipment during EVP sessions with amazing results. We noticed on one investigation while using an ionizer that activity stop. After shutting it off we asked if the tool and pointed at it, help them or hurt them? The response was it hurt them. It turns out that the ionizer built up a static charge in the skin that acted like a barrier to them. Then there was the realization that the entity was feeding off us. One of my earlier ideas was that the entity had to exist more or less like a parasite, which made since. Unfortunately, bad logic there are too many ideas of what a ghost is that sound logical on the surface. I will take the blame for this one but like the charging, the air with an ionizer to feed the ghost has been proliferated to the point of a belief. How was this equipment tested, is there any data that produced results, and where is it? Having ideas is one thing, but testing ideas is everything.

While in the Old Washoe Club in Virginia City, doing an EVP session I was hit in the arm caught on video. When reviewing the video. After I was hit, you could see the air ripple as it moved away. Describing the hit, it was more like a slap from the back of the hand in the left arm at the elbow my sleeve went up my arm moved, and you can hear the pop from the impact. At first, I thought it was a sign of aggression later after talking to a couple locals in a bar. At one time people use to live in rooms upstairs. I was told there was one person that lived there if he liked you he would slap you on the arm. You can pick up a lot of useful information and history about the location just by walking around talking to some of the locals.

Chapter 19

Easy Equipment Projects (Easily made LED Lights)

The only other pieces of equipment that is cheaper to build are Infrared LED lights. If you investigate in 'no power' conditions, I will show you how to build them in this chapter. There more powerful, use less power and cheaper than any IR light out there at a cost of $20 - $25 a depending on how many LED used in the light.

There are static charge detectors that are easy to build, but I see no practical reason for them. Since rubbing, your hands or your clothes can set them off.

Infrared LED Lights

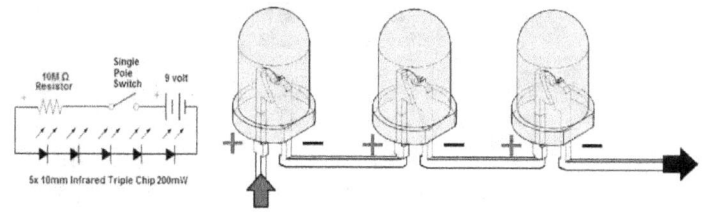

The five LED simple IR LED camera light as shown. Five LEDs from the switch + positive to - negative, I would only use 10mm Triple Chip 200mW LEDs the single chip do not last long. The project box is from Radio Shack, so is the switch. The Vivitar Hot Shoe you can find on ebay as well as the battery holder, and resistors. I would not exceed more than five LED in a strand. Strands five LED and below must have one 1k resistor the more LEDs you add in a light the need for a resistor is not necessary. Lithium batteries last 12 hours in lights built with 5 to 12 LED; there is a way by adding an IC LM555 timer to circuit that can extend battery life up to five times longer shown fig 1 below. All of these lights are very easy to build, and will save you hundreds of dollars on store bought, and custom-built lights.

I frosted the outer LEDs on this light to defuse the Infrared. The LEDs have a 30-degree lens that produces a focused spot of Infrared, so to defuse that spot I lightly sanded the lens. It gives a much more uniformed look to your videos.

You may of notice as you review your video evidence that the light slowly fades out. How you fix that is by adding an IC Voltage Regulator LM7805 to the circuit between the switch, and ground. This will give you a more consistent level of light. The lithium battery will drain completely before the light goes out.

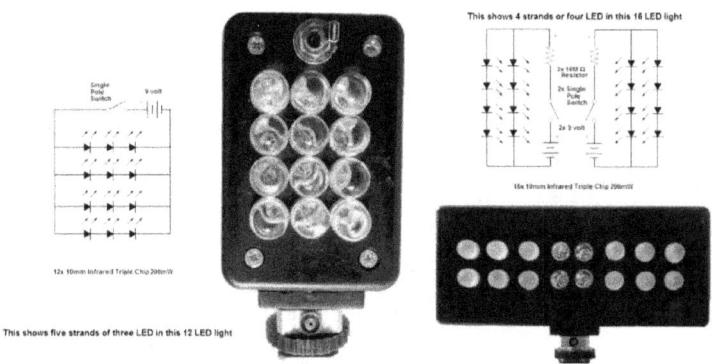

The largest light I have built was 20 Triple Chip 10mm LED that made everything look it was day.

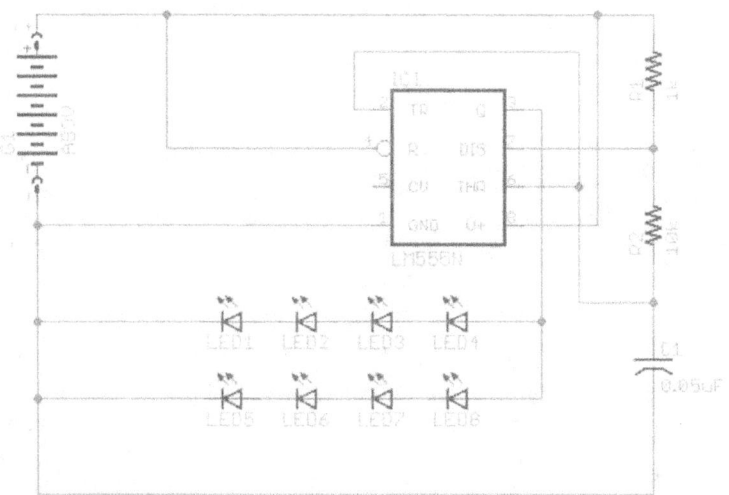

Fig1 this schematic, I use an IC LM555 precision timer to pulse the LEDs to extend battery life.

Full Spectrum

All-digital cameras are Full Spectrum the manufacture placed a filter to block ultraviolet, and infrared, all that's needed is to remove that filter from in front of the sensor, and now you see a purple-ish image. Video cameras are the same it is a good idea to replace the filter with a piece of clear photo glass if you do the modification yourself. The mods I have seen on cheap cameras really jack up the camera. One I had inspected in particular wouldn't auto focus the cameras shutter speed was set to low light, turning every bad picture that was taken in to images of ghosts! Well they wished they caught a real ghost. I have yet to see usable evidence from Full Spectrum images if only to hear some oohs and aahs from paranormal enthusiasts. You need to use a lot of light with these cameras white light would be perfect since white light contains the full light spectrum, it's cheaper, but takes away from that all needed spooky ghost hunting feeling.

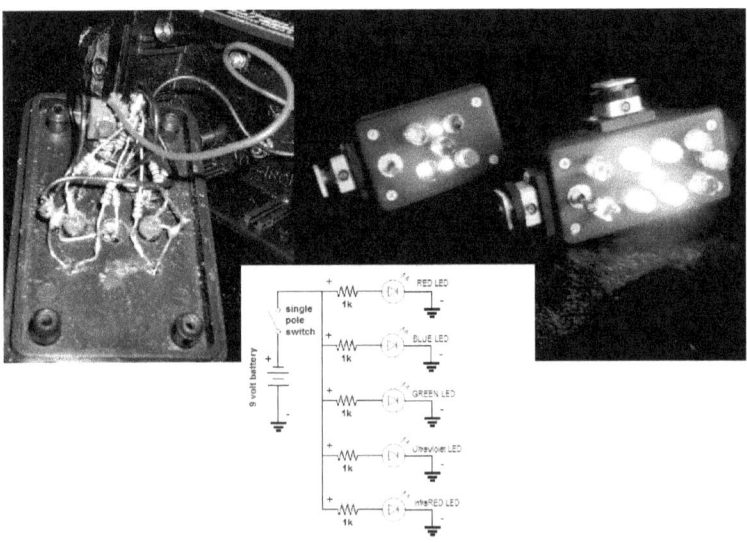

5x 10mm LED FULL SPECTRUM

Electromagnetic Field Generators
A couple very easy EM projects

The theory behind this is that the entity needs an EM field to do anything from communicating, to moving objects, and manifesting an image of its former self. Some researcher believe that the entity pulls energy from the human bio-electrical field that's generated by the heart, and open circuits that produce an EM field with its flow of electrons. There are different methods, some use ionizers statically charging the air or EM Pump to producing an EM field to "feed the Ghost". I would think providing a substantial EM field for the entity to manipulate would, and has increased activity in the manner we have use it. Each one of these project are easy to build costing $25 for the EM Pump and $39 for the Vortex EM Pump. Depending on how frugal you can get you can build these for half the price; it is up to you on how well you can find deals online.

The Vortex EM Pump

This simply is two electromagnetic fields turning into each other creating an electromagnetic funnel of sorts. Some believe that it creates an EM beacon attracting the anomaly. I have video evidence of something doing just that. You cannot see it, but you can definitely hear it come up to the camera I had it mounted on.

For both EM projects, you will need to glue the magnet up
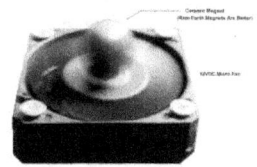
right to the top of the motor making it as centered as possible. This will keep the vibrations in the fan down reducing noise. Remember to eliminate as much noise as possible to keep from

contaminating evidence. That is why I used the fan motors because they operate quietly. That is all you need for the EM Pump one-fan motor, one magnet. The Vortex EM Pump need two fan motors with magnets one mounted on the bottom of the project box (4x2x1) spinning left to right, one mounted on the lid on the direct opposed side hanging down with a reverse spin right to left. This will spin magnetic fields into each other creating the Vortex EM field.

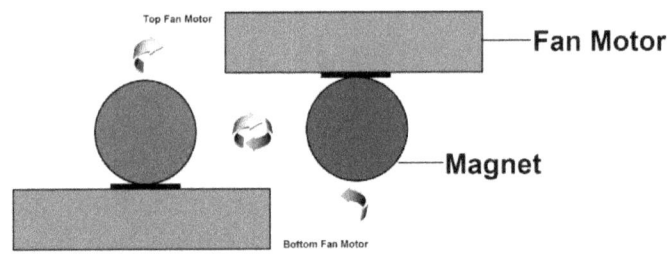

Vortex EM Pump

What you will need for the simple EM projects:

1. Single Pole Switch
2. RED LED used as a power indicator
3.12VDC Micro Fan Model: 273-240 Catalog #: 273-240
The difference between the EM Pump, and the Vortex Pump are the number of fans. Moreover, I used this fan motor because it is quiet.
4. Round Ceramic Magnet (Rare Earth Are Better)
5. Project box I used the (3x2x1") for the EM Pump, and the (4x2x1") for the EM Vortex Pump (any other sizes can be used)
6. 9 volt battery holder

How to Make an EM Pump Electronic Circuit

This EM Pump uses no magnets, and is harder to build, but is completely quiet. The cost is much less than the two examples above running around $20.

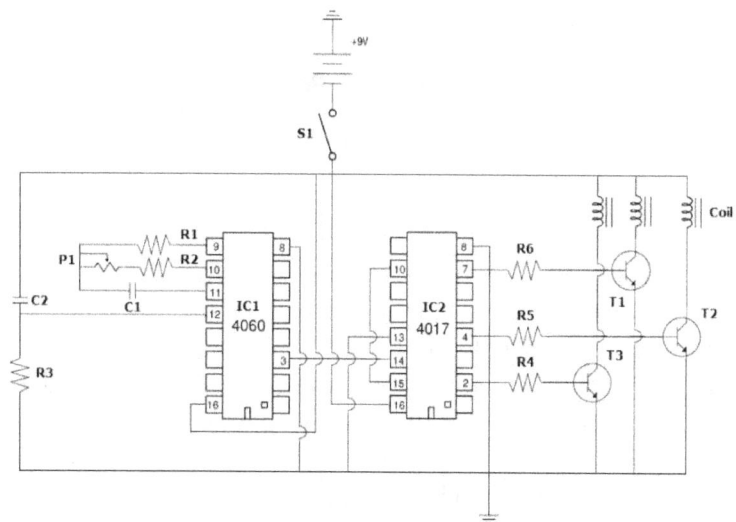

What you will need for the electronic EM project:

1. S1 = Single Pole Switch
2. R1 = 2M2
3. R2 = 1K
4. R3 = 1M
5. R4, R5, R6 = 220 OHMS
6. P1 = 100 POT
7. C1 = 10uF/16v non polar
8. C2 = 1uF
9. T1, T2, T3 = TIP122
10. IC1 = 4060
11. IC2 = 4017

How to build a Geophone

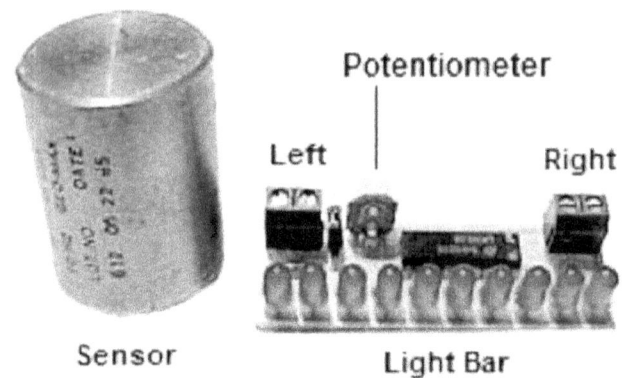

You will need to buy a Geophone Seismic Kit online, but wait until receiving it before buying the project box. The sensor is a cylinder that comes in different sizes. You will not know which size sensor they will ship with your kit until you get it. The price for these keeps going up around $30-$40 BG Micro is where I usually find the kit. Once you receive the kit, and then buy the correct size project box. The sensor shown above must mount firmly down on the base inside of the project box. Do not use glue under the base it will reduce the sensitivity of the sensor, just put glue on the sides of the cylinder. I used an aluminum project box shown above its heavier, but plastic works just fine. The light bar mounts on top; you will need to drill two holes for wiring. In image of the light bar the right side connects, the power the left side connects the sensor.

You will need to solder the wires on the sensor shown above in the top, and to the left image. The middle post usually the ground and the outer contact being the positive. This differs between manufactures of the sensor. Look for the positive side post marked as shown in the image below. I believe they still provide instructions, but I would not count on it.

The other parts you will need are a 9-volt battery holder, and push on/off switch you can find at Radio Shack.

It has a potentiometer the round white wheel next to the left wire connector in the above image. It is how you adjust the sensitivity of the device. The slightest touch near the device will register on the light bar. The adjustment is so when tapping near the surface registers two or three LEDs you do not need it so sensitive that it picks up every little vibration even though it is capable of doing so if needed.

I build and test my own equipment therefore; I have a better understanding on how my equipment works. I have not seen much in the way of equipment used, and designed for the paranormal field that has any proven purpose at all.

Only a couple things I build that are either practical or necessary, those are a couple types of EM Pump, Infrared LED lights, and Geophones. Over all these are very useful pieces of equipment.

Tablet Computers

Since the cost of a tablet computer has dropped in price that they can now manufacture them for a child of four. You can replace most of your equipment with an inexpensive

Android application that can log your data, a big advantage. Unlike the Geophone that you had to dedicate a camera to log activity. With tablet applications running on a dedicated device with simultaneous logging you now have real falsifiable data you can use to prove activity.

Chapter 20

Early Paranormal Theories

Thomas Charles Lethbridge was one of the first to promulgate the hypothesis of residual haunting. Lethbridge did so in books such as Ghost and Ghoul, written in 1961. The subject was explored in Peter Sasdy's 1972-television play, The Stone Tape, written by Nigel Kneale. The popularity of the program has led to residual haunting become known colloquially as the "Stone Tape theory."

Stone Tape Theory is a paranormal hypothesis that was proposed in the 1970s as a possible explanation for ghosts. It speculates that inanimate materials can absorb some form of energy from living beings; the hypothesis speculates that this 'recording' happens especially during moments of high tension, such as murder, or during intense moments of one's life. This stored energy can be released at any given moment, resulting in a display of the occurred activity. According to this hypothesis, ghosts are not spirits at all, but simply non-interactive recordings, similar to a movie. Thomas Charles was one of the first to promulgate the hypothesis of residual haunting.

Electromagnetic Field Theory: EMF is a force given off by electric charges the force is evident in nearly everything in nature. Both living and non-living or inanimate devices emit an electromagnetic field. The higher the spikes in the electromagnetic field, the more potential there is for paranormal activity. The theory is that a ghost or spirit gives off an electromagnetic field, which detected by Electromagnetic Field meters. A paranormal occurrence or ghost may give off Milligauss readings in the range of 1.5 mG to about 6 mG, depending on the EMF meter you use. If you get a paranormal reading, the reading should not be a steady. Steady constant reading is usually artificial in nature.

Fear Cage Theory: This is a confined or localized area with unhealthily high levels of electromagnetic radiation due to the presence of a large amount of electrical devices, unshielded electrical cables, or power junctions.
Individuals with sensitivity to Electromagnetic Fields (EMF) can experience sensations of anxiety, paranoia, or nausea after prolonged exposure to these places. Some also report feelings of "being watched." The effect often gives rise to sincere but unsubstantiated claims of haunting.

Electronic Voice Phenomena Theory: EVP refers to voices that appear on recording devices (such as tape recorders) with no apparent source. Swedish film producer, Friedrich Juergenson, while recording bird song in a forest for an upcoming movie, first discovered the phenomenon. He heard two very faint but audible voices while playing back the recording he had made through a reel-to-reel machine. The first was the voice of a man speaking of the bird song at night, and the other was that of his mother calling him by his nickname and saying he was being watched over.

Water Theory: Running water can store an immense amount of kinetic energy. Saltwater is a very good conductor of electricity. Fresh water is also a conductor, but not a very good one. An abundant energy source, such as a body of water, can lend its energy to intensifying paranormal activity.

Imprinting Theory (Haunted Objects): An entity can attach its energy to an item of a personal nature, imprinting itself on the object. The energy imprint can remain, though objects are moved long distances...see Residual Haunting

Full Moon Theory: (Full Moons, Thunderstorms, Solar Flares) the phases of the moon have an effect on the geomagnetic field. Most paranormal investigators believe that the geomagnetic fields are strongest at the full moon and the new moon phases, causing paranormal activity to intensify. Under the theory, the best time to conduct an investigation is two to three days prior to a full or new moon or two to three days after a full or new moon. It is believed that ghosts draw their energy through electrical resources. During solar x-rays and geomagnetic storms, the air filled with electricity from which spirits draw energy.

Note: It is also convenient for paid venues to raise the price during the full moon. Even though there is no proof that it makes any difference at all.

Conscious Energy Theory – by Edward Krietemeyer

In 1968, the case studies of Dr. Celia Green that associated some types of psychological stress, extreme fear, and physical trauma could trigger an Out of Body Experience OBE. Medical science is conducting a three-year study of Near Death Experience NDE that our human conscious triggered by death itself can extend outside its physical host called the awareness.

If our bioelectrical consciousness has the ability to extend outside of its physical host induce by trauma. Then death would be the method of breaking the connection to our physical host.

Our conscious-self would exist by imprinting, or anchoring itself to a suitable substrate, feeding off the physical in a limited existence similar to a parasite. Influencing the physical world by manipulating its yet unknown properties.

References

Chapter: 1
Human Consciousness Project Breakthroughs in the science of what happens when we die. (Online Article)
The Human Consciousness Project (The AWARE Study)

Chapter: 2
Darkness, Silence Cause Hallucinations
By Adam Smith / STAFF WRITER
Drugs.com provides accurate and independent information on more than 24,000 prescription drugs (Online)
Los Angeles Times article Caffeine linked to hallucinations in study, but have another cup of coffee anyway June 08, 2011|By Chris Woolston, HealthKey / For the Booster Shots blog.

Chapter: 3
Hepa Filters and Air Filtration Systems for a Variety of Contamination Control Applications (Online)
FS209E and ISO Cleanroom Standards
How many skin cells do you shed every day?
(p1, 2, 3)
Exchangeable image file format EXIF
Pareidolia quote
Ideomotor Effect quote
Wikimedia Foundation, Inc.

Chapter: 4
Electronics Basics: What Is Alternating Current?
By Doug Lowe from Electronics All-In-One Desk Reference for Dummies. (Online Article)

Chapter: 5
Carl Sagan THE DEMON-HAUNTED WORLD quote:
(p 287)
Neil deGrasse Tyson from Cosmos: A Spacetime Odyssey

Chapter: 8
A Two-Year Investigation of the Allegedly
Anomalous Electronic Voices or EVP
NeuroQuantology | September 2012 | Volume 10 | Issue 3 |
Page 492-514 Cardoso A., Anomalous electronic voices
Formant Wikimedia Foundation, Inc.
Ladefoged's A Course in Phonetics
How do I read a spectrogram?
Rob Hagiwara (Online)

Chapter: 9
Thomas Edison and the Ghost in the Machine
Paranormal-encyclopedia.com
Voice Transmissions with the Deceased
By Friedrich Jürgenson
Breakthrough: An Amazing Experiment in Electronic
Communication with the Dead
By Konstantin Raudive, Ph.D. (1971)
Konstantīns Raudive
Wikimedia Foundation, Inc.
A Two-Year Investigation of the Allegedly
Anomalous Electronic Voices or EVP
NeuroQuantology | September 2012 | Volume 10 | Issue 3 |
Page 492-514
Cardoso A., Anomalous electronic voices

Chapter: 10
Dog – Vision Wikimedia Foundation, Inc.

Chapter: 13
Mysteries at the Museum Presents Annabelle (YouTube)
Robert the Doll Wikimedia Foundation, Inc. (Online)
Ghost Stories (Online)
Collection of stories about paranormal phenomena.
Mandy the Doll

Chapter: 16
Four Dimensional Being
Princeton University quote
Three-dimensional world video (YouTube)
By Dr. Michio Kaku, professor of theoretical physics at City
College of New York

The websites of CGC - Ghost Chasing Need to Know Blog,
and The Institute of Spectrological Research website -
Institute of Spectrological Research Blog.

Glossary of Terms

A

Active: Ongoing reported claims of a haunting or unexplained paranormal phenomenon.

Anomaly: A strange occurrence that cannot be rationalized by objective critical scientific evaluation.

Anthropomorphism is any attribution of human characteristics (or characteristics assumed to belong only to humans) to animals, non-living things, phenomena, material states, objects or abstract concepts, such as spirits or deities. The term coined in the mid-1700s. Examples include animals, plants, and forces of nature such as winds, rain or the sun depicted as creatures with human motivations, and/or the abilities to reason and converse.

Apophenia is the experience of seeing meaningful patterns or connections in random or meaningless data.

Astral Plane: A world that believed to exist above our physical world.

Astral Projection: See Out-of-body experience.

Aura: Refers to the energy field emanating from the surface of a person or object. This emanation visualized as an outline of cascading color and may be held to represent soul vibrations, chakra emergence, or a reflection of surrounding energy fields.

Audio Pareidolia: see Apophenia

Anomalous Voice Phenomenon (AVP): See Electronic Voice Phenomenon (EVP)

Acoustical Voice Phenomenon (AVP): See Electronic Voice Phenomenon (EVP)
Both has minor variations in meaning which has to do with more the characteristics, and properties of the anomaly.

Anomalous: Is more accepted in mainstream science.

B

Bioelectromagnetism: (sometimes equated with bioelectricity) refers to the electrical, magnetic or electromagnetic fields produced by living cells, tissues or organisms. Examples include the cell membrane potential and the electric currents that flow in nerves and muscles, because of action potentials.

Biofield: See Bioelectromagnetism

C

Case Study: An in-depth investigation of an individual subject.

Control: This is a procedure in paranormal psychology that ensures that the experiment is conducted in a standard fashion so that the results will not be influenced by any extraneous factors.

Control Group: A group of outside subjects whose performance or abilities are compared with the experimental subjects.

Corona: A type of plasma "atmosphere" of the Sun or other celestial body, extending millions of kilometers into space, most easily seen during a total solar eclipse, but also observable in a coronagraph. The Latin root of the word corona means crown.

Crisis Apparition: An apparition that is seen when a person is seriously ill, seriously injured or at the point of death.

D

Decibel originates from methods used to quantify reductions in audio levels in telephone circuits. These losses originally measured in units of Miles of Standard Cable seldom-used unit named in honor of Alexander Graham Bell.

> **dB** is not based on a unit of measurement but a scale of amplitude.

> **dBm** power of sound in watts = 0.001 (one mill watt)

Doppelgänger: An existence of a spirit doubles, or ghosts an exact but usually invisible replica of a living person or any other sort of physical double. Seeing one's own doppelgänger is an omen of death.

Demonology: Religious teaching from a seminary, or Bible College. Based on Christion beliefs to combat demons, or possessed people or locations of evil spirits. There are no accredited courses to become a demonologist.

E

Electromagnetic Field (EMF): A measurable field of electrical energy. Some believe that anomalous shifts in the electromagnetic field can be evidence of a ghost attempting to manifest. Others believe that ghosts are drawn to high-level electromagnetic fields.

Electromagnetic Field Meter (EMF Meter): Electricians' use these meters to check for bad wiring, and are typically calibrated to detect frequencies within the range of alternating current from the factory. Therefor testing and recalibrating these devices are not possible or a requirement for an electricians' tool dealing with typical 110 - 240 volts from an US household outlet. Scientific devices to ensure the accuracy of the data must be tested, and recalibrated each time it is used.

As this book focuses on what is explainable the practicality of using these devices. After once we understand how these devises work, knowing that flashy lights look good on television. In all reality serves no purpose outside of its intended use.

Electronic Voice Phenomenon (EVP): A form of Instrumental Trans-Communication wherein human ears, but are do not immediately hear anomalous disembodied voices and sounds noticed recording equipment or other electronics designed to capture or transfer sound that can be listened to later.

Entity: Intelligent, parasitic, energy-based life forms that can possess or inhabit a physical life form to control it and feed off its life force until the host die. Also, see Ghost.

F

Falsifiable: confirmable: capable of being tested (verified or falsified) by experiment or observation.

Fear Cage: A confined or localized area with unhealthily high levels of electromagnetic radiation due to the presence of a large amount of electrical devices, unshielded electrical cables, or power junctions. Individuals with sensitivity to Electromagnetic Fields (EMF) can experience sensations of anxiety, paranoia, or nausea after prolonged exposure to these places. They report feelings of "being watched" and this effect often gives rise to sincere but unsubstantiated claims of haunting.

Fortean: Pertaining to extraordinary and strange phenomenon and happenings, 1970s: from the name of Charles H. Fort (1874–1932), American student of paranormal phenomena.

G

Ghost: Disembodied pattern of Electromagnetic Energy that interacts with the material world in a seemingly intelligent, patterned, or organized manner.

H

Haunting: A state of being wherein research and evaluation cannot explain away multiple consistent anomalous occurrences and a conclusion is drawn that certain events taking place at or about the location are of paranormal origin.

Haunted house: Defined as a house that believed to be a center for supernatural occurrences or paranormal phenomena.

Hertz unit of frequency defined as the number of cycles per second, and named for Heinrich Rudolf Hertz.

Hz is the unit of measurement for frequencies.

I

Intelligent Entity: A supernatural being that evidences intelligence and will of its own.

Intelligent Haunting: This type of haunt is when the entity is aware of the living world and interacts with or responds to it. The entity is able to communicate with the living, not just by talking, but also by moving inanimate objects such as furniture or other objects.

JKL

M

Matrixing: Tendency for the human mind to interpret sensory input (that which is perceived visually, audibly or physically) as something familiar or more easily understood, accepted, and in effect is mentally "filling in the blanks".

Milligauss – 1 gauss = 1 Mx/cm2 this unit is named after Carl Friedrich Gauss.

> **mG** = Milligauss – a unit of measurement of a magnetic field equal to one thousandth of 1 gauss.
>
> **mV** = millivolt - a unit of potential equal to one thousandth of a volt.

N

Near Death Experience (NDE): An experience that has reported by people who clinically die, or come close to actual death and are revived. These events often include encounters with spirit guides, seeing dead relatives or friends, life review, out-of-body-experiences (OBE), or a moment of decision where they are able to decide or told to turn back.

O

Orbs: Assumed to be a sign of paranormal activity, but is nothing more than an optical anomaly consisting of dust, bugs, or other particulate matter, including moisture.

Out-of-body experience (OBE): A sensation or experience in which one self or spirit travels to a different location than their physical body.

P

Paranatural: See Paranormal

Paranormal: A general term that designates experiences that lie outside "the range of normal experience or scientific explanation", or which indicate phenomena understood to be outside of science's current ability to explain or measure.

Paranormal phenomena are distinct from certain hypothetical entities, coupled with observation and scientific methodology.

Paranormal Entity: Any being that modern science has not officially recorded or classified.

Paranormal Investigation: The practice of going to a location where accounts of paranormal activity have been reported and working to investigate, rationalize, and/or document those specific claims.

Paranormal Investigator: A person who investigates or researches the activity of paranormal entities.

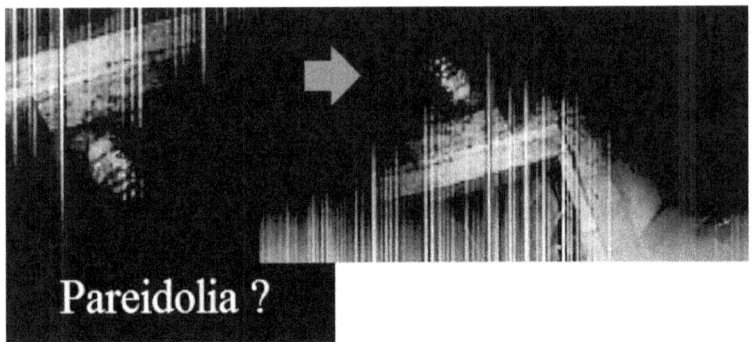

Pareidolia ?

A psychological phenomenon involving a vague and random stimulus (often an image or sound) being perceived as significant. Common examples include seeing images of animals or faces in clouds, and hearing hidden messages on records played in reverse.

Peer Review: A group of colleague's and experts that professionally evaluate a body of work.

Phantom Smell: Anomalous odors, with no definable source, that can be smelled by unaided normal human olfactory senses.

Phantom Sound: Anomalous sounds, with no definable source, that can be heard by unaided normal human auditory senses.

Phantom Touch: The anomalous sensation of being physically touched, despite no physical contact being made with a material being or object.

Phonology: Study of linguistics that deals with systems of sounds comprised in language.

Phonetics & Phonology: Study of the production of sounds that comprise speech by the articulatory and vocal tract.

Preternatural: Beyond what is normal or natural

Pseudo-science: A methodology, belief, or practice that claimed to be scientific, or that is made to appear to be scientific, but which does not adhere to an appropriate scientific methodology, lacks supporting evidence or plausibility, or otherwise lacks scientific status.

Psychic: A person (also called a sensitive) who professes an ability to perceive information hidden from the normal senses through extrasensory perception, or is said by others to have such abilities.

Physical Manifestation: Situation wherein a supernatural entity physically appears in a manner visible to unaided normal human visual senses.

Psychokinetic Activity: The anomalous event of inanimate physical objects being moved without interacting with a material entity or other discernible mundane source that would cause movement.

Psycho-kinesis: The ability to unconsciously control objects with only the mind.

Q

R

Residual Entity: A supernatural being that evidences no intelligence or will of its own, and simply acts out the same scene or pattern of behavior repeatedly until the pattern fades away.

Residual Haunt: It is nothing more than an echo of past events playing repeatedly until the pattern fades away.
Unlike an intelligent haunting, it does not directly involve a spiritual anomaly aware of the living world and interacting with or responding to it.

S

Scientific Theory: A theory that explains scientific observations, "scientific theories must be falsifiable" A scientific theory differs from any form of theory, which is defined as:

1. A tentative theory about the natural world; a concept that is not yet verified but that, if true, would explain certain facts or phenomena.

2. A belief that can guide behavior; "The architect has a theory that more is less"; "They killed him, based on the theory that dead men tell no tales." Thus, any idea can be called a "theory," but a scientific theory is more narrowly defined as something that explains a natural phenomenon and provides testable predictions that can be "falsifiable" (i.e., "proven false").

Sensitive: See Psychic

Séance: A séance is an attempt to communicate with spirits. The word came to be used specifically for a meeting of people who gathered to receive messages from spirits or to listen to a spirit mediums' discourse with or relay messages from spirits. Like the Ouija Board, this works on the principle that the group's intentions are to contact spirits. The users cannot control what comes through are sometimes doorways or portals that can be opened that allow other spirits through. See Table Tipping

Simulacrum: Abstraction today is no longer that of the map, the double, the mirror or the concept. Simulation is no longer that of a territory, a referential being or a substance. It is the generation by models of a real without origin or reality: a hyper-real.

- A slight, unreal, or superficial likeness or semblance.
- Psychosomatic: It is a question of substituting the real as signs of the real.

Spectrum Analysis: Software used by sound engineers to measure the magnitude of an input signal by its frequency components in a visual representation.

Spectrological: The study of Ghosts

Supernatural Entity: See Paranormal Entity

T

Table Tipping: Also known as, "Table Turning "is another type of séance, in which participants sit around a table, place their hands on it, and wait for the table to levitate or wobble back and forth. The table was a means of communicating with the spirits, or to show that a spirit is present in the room.

TAPS: The Atlantic Paranormal Society founded by Jason Hawes, and Grant Wilson. Featured on the SyFy-reality TV series Ghost Hunters a production of Pilgrim Films.

Traditional Haunting: See Intelligent Haunting

UV

W

Witching hour: A term for the time of night when ghosts are the most active usually placed at between midnight and 3am.

White noise brown noise pink noise: Is noises containing many different frequencies, at equal intensity. Used by paranormal teams to enhance Electronic Voice Phenomenon EVP collection.

XYZ

Paranormal • Belief • Mind • Books • Research

Culture & Science • Afterlife • Ghost • History

Education

www.ingramcontent.com/pod-product-compliance
Lightning Source LLC
Chambersburg PA
CBHW070901290526

45795CB00001B/198